A SENSE
OF BETRAYAL
RECOLLECTIONS OF VIETNAM

BY
DAVID RITCHEY
WITH HARPER SCHANTZ

Headline Books, Inc.
Terra Alta, WV

A Sense of Betrayal

by David Ritchey

To order additional copies of the book, or to contact the author:
Headline Books, Inc.
P O Box 52
Terra Alta, WV 26764

www.HeadlineBooks.com
www.DavidRitchey.com

ISBN-13: 978-0-938467-51-9

Library of Congress Control Number:

Ritchey, David
A sense of betrayal
    p. cm.
        ISBN 978-0-938467-51-9
1. Vietnam 2. US Government 3. Veterans
  Non-Fiction

To my daughter Harper, my son Mac,
and to their mother, Elaine,
all of whose lives were significantly changed
as a result of my experiences in Vietnam.

CONTENTS

PREFACE

While this is a book about war, it is not a tale of blood, guts, and glory. It's ironic, isn't it, that the word "glory" is used in association with the words "blood" and "guts," when a much more appropriate association would be with the word "horror?" In my personal experience of war, I was sufficiently far removed from the "down and dirty" fighting that I didn't encounter a whole lot in the way of "blood and guts." Never once, for example, did I see an American body that wasn't already in a body bag. While I did see several enemy bodies, I had learned to think of them as something less than human, so the sight of their blood and guts wasn't particularly impactful on me. I did, however, experience my share of the psychological horrors of war, and those horrors are what I address in this book.

The main body of the book's text deals with my recollections of my experiences as a naval officer in Vietnam. Experiences are based on perceptions and, given the fallibility of both perception and memory, even under ordinary circumstances, there are likely to be any number of instances in which the information

I provide may not be completely accurate historically. Much of what I have written here is based on letters I wrote when I was in Vietnam; that does not, however, insure the accuracy of the information because at the time I had a very limited understanding of "the big picture." For me, and I suspect for most others who were doing the fighting, it seemed like the entire war was being fought within the narrow confines of the area for which we were responsible, and nothing else seemed to be of any real import. I have done the relevant research wherever practical, but I regularly encountered conflicting data, so many of the "facts" I present need to be taken with a grain of salt.

Some of the terms I use were specific to the war in Vietnam, and may be familiar only to those of us who served there, so I have included them in the glossary. Additionally, there were many cases in which we were expected to speak of events using language that obfuscated their true meaning. Illustratively, River Patrol Boat (PBR) ambushes were supposed to be called "waterborne guard posts," the My Lai Massacre was supposed to be called the "My Lai Incident," and the invasion of Cambodia was supposed to be called the "Cambodian Campaign." These euphemisms, I suppose, were intended to make the events less abhorrent to the American public, but I could never quite bring myself to use the "appropriate" terms.

My objective in setting out to write this book was primarily one of attempting to better understand the actions, and what motivated those actions, of the senior military officers and politicians of both the United States and South Vietnam. It didn't take much time serving in Vietnam for me to realize that, while the men I was responsible for were putting their lives on the line, the senior military officers and politicians of both countries, for the sake of what I call "the 4 P's,"— Power, Prestige, Position, and Pelf (money)—would not hesitate to betray those men. I was dismayed, and resolved to do my best to maintain my own honor and integrity within a system that had none. Sometimes I succeeded; sometimes I didn't.

I am enough of a realist to recognize that the dynamics I observed were not unique to the war in Vietnam, that they probably are characteristic of all wars, in all locales, and in all eras. Despite the disillusionment I feel as a result of my experience of the sociodynamics of which I became aware in Vietnam, I still have enough idealism left to hope that by writing about those dynamics I can bring them to people's conscious awareness, and possibly even help to effect some modicum of constructive change in the future. More than 40 years have elapsed since I served in Vietnam, but it seems like only yesterday, and many of the emotions I have relative to my experiences are still quite raw. Not wanting to reopen old emotional wounds, I have taken a rather detached, objective stance in writing the story I have to tell. Detachment and objectivity were also effective instinctual coping mechanisms for dealing with those experiences as they occurred, and helped me to maintain a relatively intact psyche. It is my hope that you, the reader, might be able to use the insights I offer to somehow contribute to effecting positive change in our world of perpetual conflict.

I want to extend my acknowledgement and thanks to my daughter, Harper Schantz, who so fully gave of herself in helping me to edit the original manuscript. She also wrote a very enlightening Afterword that provides a different perspective, and offers valuable insight into how the Vietnam War affected her, a representative of those who were the children of those of us who served.

INTRODUCTION

"It shook his faith in civilization and civilized man. It made him mordantly conscious of how thin the veneer of civilization really was, and of that point of no return beyond which men fell...into satanic depths... He had seen how, under pressure and removed from customary restraints, even the most [civilized of men] could give way to destructive impulses rising from the depths of their own natures: unbridled vanity, greed, and appetite for power that, in its extreme form, swells into the desire to play God. ... [His experiences] had taught him that the world was a dangerous place ... and an even more disturbing lesson: how dangerous men were."

The above quotation, from the introduction to Joseph Conrad's *Heart of Darkness*, speaks to the way in which the book's main character, Marlow's, journey into the heart of imperialist Africa affected his perceptions of the world and the society in which he lived. It also speaks to the way in which my journey into the heart of Vietnam affected my perceptions of the world, and the society in which I live. This theme, the recognition of human capacities for evil and the superficial nature of human moral systems, is not uncommon in literature throughout the ages.

~ ~ ~

The war in Vietnam was characterized by lies, deceits, manipulations, and betrayals of "what's right," perpetrated by our allies, by our military, and by our government. Even the Gulf of Tonkin incidents of August 1964, which opened the door for full-scale American combat operations in Vietnam, were lacking in credibility. The first event on August 2nd, in which the American destroyer, the USS Maddox, was attacked by North Vietnamese torpedo boats, was apparently genuine. It was the second "attack" on August 4th, however, that led to the passage of the Gulf of Tonkin Resolution. That incident served as President Lyndon Johnson's legal justification for deploying conventional forces, and the commencement of open warfare against North Vietnam. Subsequent research has indicated, with almost total certainty, that the second attack never really happened. President Johnson and his advisors had been desperately seeking a pretext for direct and vigorous military action, and this bogus incident served their purposes well.

It was often stated that the over-riding purpose of the Vietnam War was one of bringing democracy to Southeast Asia, but that wasn't really the case. The war was not so much about promoting democracy as it was about promoting anti-communism—an entirely different objective. While the enemy was fighting an all-out war of national liberation, with the objective of defeating us, we were fighting a limited war in which we did not seek a clear-cut victory, but rather a negotiated, compromise peace. We were also not fighting a war of territorial objectives, but rather one of attrition in which we hoped the enemy, after we inflicted sufficiently large losses of manpower, would eventually be unable to recover and would simply give up. That was wishful thinking on our part. The enemy had an extraordinary will to persist, could absorb losses unthinkable to us Americans, and was quickly able to recover from any damage we inflicted. Illustratively, it has been estimated that the North Vietnamese Army and the Vietcong suffered the loss of approximately 1,100,000 troops killed in action. When adjusted for the difference in population size between Vietnam and the United States, that is the equivalent of having 5 – 10 million U.S. troops killed. We, in fact, lost "only" about 58,000 troops during the entire war, but that was more than our national psyche was able to tolerate. Those 58,000 deaths can further be put into perspective by noting that the average number of automobile deaths per year in the United States for the period of 1962 to 1972 was about 49,000.

The relatively low number of U.S. deaths was, at least in part, a result of the policy of "expend munitions, not lives." We dropped seven million tons of bombs in Vietnam, as compared to a total of two million tons dropped by the allies in all of World War II. That works out to be 350 pounds of bombs for every man, woman and child in all of Vietnam. The financial cost of this policy was considerable. According to one estimate, it cost the United States $9.60 for every dollar of damage the air war inflicted on North Vietnam. According to another estimate, the cost of killing one Viet Cong was $400,000. But the policy did save American lives. In spite of all that, we lost the war. It was the only war that the United States had ever lost, and the impact on the national psyche was devastating. We could no longer think of ourselves as being "invincible," and the fact that we could be defeated by a third-rate military power was almost beyond comprehension.

The young servicemen sent to protect America from the Communist menace didn't encounter John Wayne heroics. What they encountered were "free-fire zones," "recon by fire," "search and destroy," and "body counts"—the long and dismal array of atrocities that constituted American policy in Vietnam. In short, they encountered compelling evidence of "man's inhumanity to man." Disillusionment among the troops became rampant, as evidenced by heavy drug use, "fragging" (the killing of superior officers with fragmentation grenades), an unprecedented number of desertions (most of which did not take place under fire, indicating that they were caused by disgust rather than fear), and "combat refusals" (a euphemism for "mutiny"). All of this took its psychological toll on the troops and it has been estimated that, among those who served in Vietnam, as many as 30%—that is, one million servicemen—eventually suffered from what is now known as Post-Traumatic Stress Disorder (PTSD). One result of this is that more Vietnam Veterans have died of suicide than died on the battlefields during the entire war. It is germane to note here that, at an average age of 20, the soldiers were 6 years younger than their fathers who fought in World War II—and their youth presumably contributed to their susceptibility to PTSD. Even today, 40 years later, the Vietnam War continues to take its toll in alcoholism, drug abuse, depression, and suicide.

After the Tet Offensive in the spring of 1968, in which the enemy demonstrated its strength and commitment to its cause, and in which the lying of the American government was brought into focus, the mood of the American public turned against the war and those who served in it. Vietnam Veterans, upon returning home, were shunned and denigrated. Those who opposed the war vilified them as "baby killers," and those who still supported the war derided them as "losers." The public's faith in the government, and the honesty and competence of its leaders, was significantly undermined. The American populace developed a high degree of suspicion and distrust toward authority of any kind—a distrust that continues to this day. Two popular bumper stickers of the time illustrate the point: The first was "Question Authority"; the second was, "I Love My Country, But Fear My Government." The betrayal of the Vietnam Veterans was exacerbated by the Veterans' Administration that did virtually nothing to help those who were incapacitated by Agent Orange, PTSD, alcoholism, drug abuse, depression, and suicide. After the conclusion of the war, the majority of Americans neither wanted to talk about it nor to think about it— thus further isolating the Vietnam Veterans and also setting the stage for a repeat performance in the future.

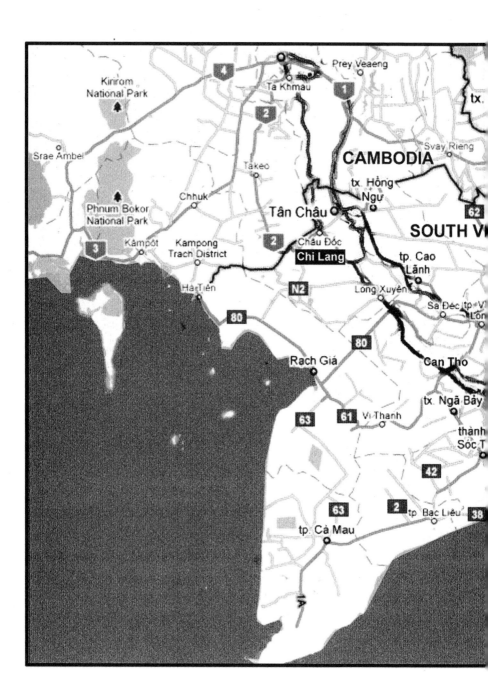

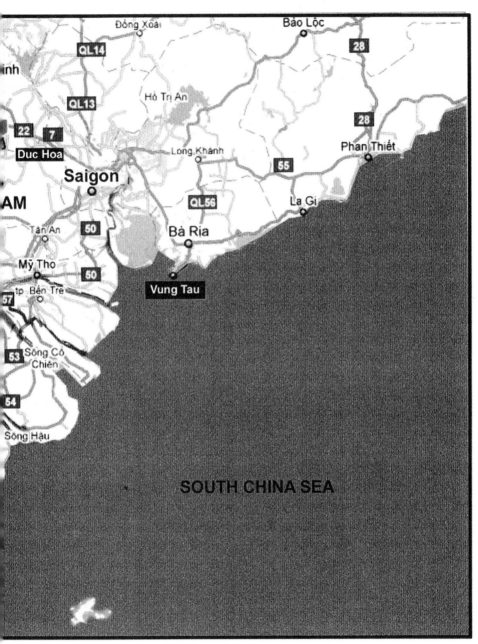

Map of III Corps & IV Corps, South Vietnam,
showing Vung Tau, Chi Lang, Duc Hoa

CHAPTER 1
STATESIDE
(MAY 1968 – MARCH 1969)

Technically, the United States' involvement in the war in Vietnam began in 1961. Even though I was then in Navy ROTC, and later in the United States Navy proper, I didn't pay much attention to Vietnam for several years. All of that changed for me in the fall of 1968.

I was then a young Navy Lieutenant assigned to a new-construction destroyer escort being built by the Lockheed Corporation in Seattle. The ship had an experimental engineering plant for which I was responsible, and for which I had extensive specialized training. I was scheduled for normal rotation to a new assignment in October of that year, but during the summer both my Captain and I requested that the Bureau of Naval Personnel extend my assignment to the ship. We were both led to believe that our requests had been accepted...but then, in the military, one can't count on anything.

In September, I had my annual military physical examination at the local Navy hospital. Shortly thereafter, a special report about the results of that examination was misrouted, and ended up on my desk rather than going directly to the doctors at the hospital. Given that it was about me, I checked it out carefully and found that it was full of medical jargon having to do with scar tissue on my lungs. I went to the hospital and asked for an explanation, but was told that none would be forthcoming because it was "none of my business." I was dumbfounded—my lungs were none of my business? Muddling in my bewilderment, I felt that those whose jobs were supposed to involve ensuring my medical well-being had violated my trust. Attempting to work through my confusion and frustration, I ended up going to a civilian internist who ran a number of tests and informed me that since I tested negative for tuberculosis, the only logical explanation was that I must have, at some point, contracted "San Joaquin Valley Fever." When I told him that I had never been near the San Joaquin Valley, he said we could only chalk it up as an unexplained medical mystery.

Twenty-five years later, when I was doing research on biological warfare weapons, I discovered that the U.S. Navy had been testing one such weapon, known as "coccidiomycosis" on unsuspecting naval personnel at the Philadelphia Naval Shipyard in 1966. Well, "coccidiomycosis" and "San Joaquin Valley Fever" are one and the same thing, and I had been stationed at the Philadelphia Naval Shipyard during the summer of 1966. It seemed pretty clear that I had been one of those unwitting test subjects. My sense of having been betrayed by the military medical system was complete, and I was outraged.

Given that my term of obligated active duty was due to expire in June of 1969, I wrote to the Bureau Of Naval Personnel in October of 1968, submitting my resignation. Their response was prompt and pointed. I was informed that the extension of my assignment aboard the destroyer escort was cancelled, that my obligated time in service was being involuntarily extended, and that I would be sent to Vietnam. Again, I felt a sense of betrayal.

In December, I received secret orders to the U.S. Army Intelligence School at Fort Holabird Maryland. Those orders, which arrived at the start of the Christmas holidays, gave me no idea what to expect other than that I was to wear civilian clothes, and they required that I report on January 2nd, 1969. My family and I were thrown into chaos. We had to forgo celebrating Christmas, and had only ten days to get all our possessions crated and put into storage, sell our car, fly from the West Coast to Baltimore, get another car, and find a place to live. Because we had so little time, we had to settle for a dreadful apartment in a run-down section of Baltimore. We then had to scramble to buy winter clothes, bed and bath linens, and all of the necessities and toys for our little one. My wife spent much of her time in tears, and so did our daughter.

~ ~ ~

At the intelligence school, on the first day of class, the Commanding Officer of the school told us that, while we were all "volunteers," and that we knew what we were getting into, he wanted to remind us that we were going to be trained in "black intelligence." He advised us that our training would involve those aspects of intelligence that were illegal under international law—the Geneva Conventions, the Nuremberg Principles, and such—that the U.S. government would not stand behind us if our activities were to come to light, and that if we had any reservations about performing such duties, we were to request withdrawal immediately.

I had many reservations, indeed, but thought I would give it a couple of weeks to see if we were just being subjected to meaningless scare tactics. We weren't. We were taught about the fine art of lying, deceit, and manipulation; we were taught about assassination and torture; we were taught about how to avoid getting found out. Ludicrously, we were sent into the slums of Baltimore to surreptitiously deliver and retrieve messages, to follow people, and to spy—ludicrous because, given our stature, bearing, and haircuts, we were obviously in the military and couldn't be surreptitious about anything because we stood out like sore thumbs.

I very quickly came to realize that this was duty for which I was clearly unsuited, and I wasn't about to volunteer for an assignment where it had been clearly stated, up front, that my own government wouldn't hesitate to abandon me. I therefore requested withdrawal. The Army readily accepted my request, but the Navy's position was quite different. I was confined to quarters pending court martial for my refusal to obey orders— so much for a "voluntary" assignment. I felt I definitely could not trust the system, that the Navy and the Government had become "the enemy," and, with feelings of great desperation, I considered relocating to Canada as a way out of this situation. Other than from my wife, I received no support whatsoever from the rest of my family, and felt very much alone. The Navy, however, ultimately came up with an acceptable solution to our impasse. I was ordered to a position as a Coastal Surveillance Center watch officer in Vietnam, a position for which I was well trained, and one that didn't violate my moral principles, so I accepted those orders.

Struggling to deal with record snowfalls, I got my family settled in, north of Boston, and then boarded a plane to Vietnam. The mood of the troops on board the plane was positive, upbeat, and energetic. It was almost like being at a pep rally before a football game. Most of us had no idea what we were getting into; most of us still had absolute faith in our Government; and most of us were eagerly anticipating the opportunity to become heroes. The plane eventually landed at Cam Ranh Bay, which was the headquarters of the Coastal Surveillance Force.

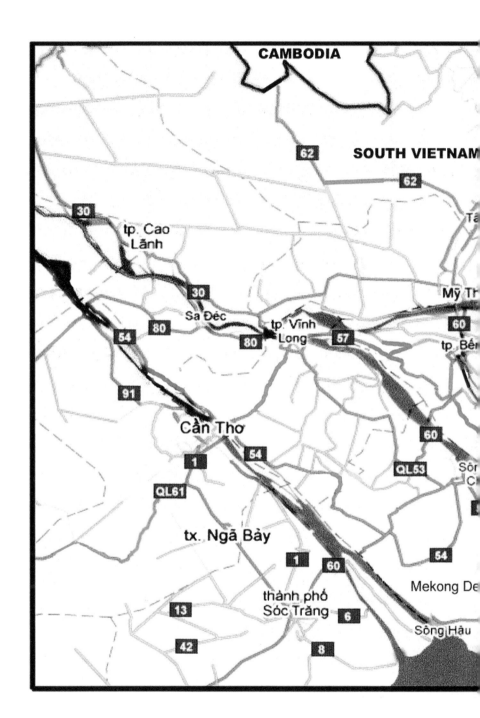

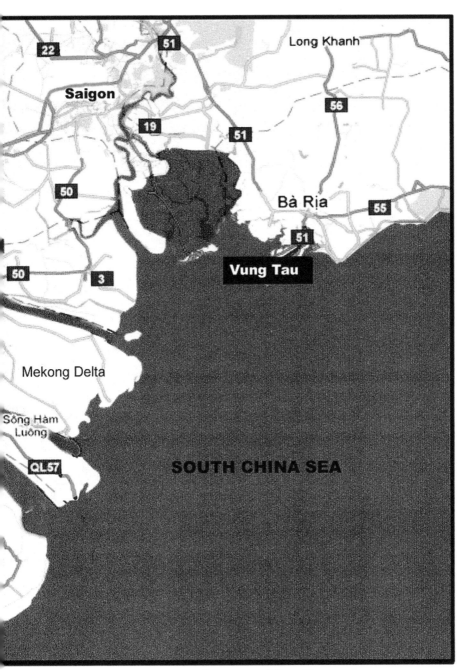

Map of area around Vung Tau,
South Vietnam including Mekong River Delta

CHAPTER 2
VUNG TAU
(MARCH 1969 – SEPTEMBER 1969)

From Cam Rahn Bay, I flew the 200 miles southwest to the city of Vung Tau where I would take on the duties of a Coastal Surveillance Force watch officer. "City" is perhaps not the right term to describe Vung Tau. Even in wartime, it was more like a lovely tropical seaside resort town with miles of beautiful beaches, lush jungle foliage, beautiful tropical flowers, and a very active nightlife. Vung Tau was located on a peninsula, Cape Saint Jacques, extending into the South China Sea, only 70 miles from Saigon. With a population of about 100,000, its economy was centered on fishing and tourism.

Fortuitously, Vung Tau was recognized by both sides in the war as a superb location for "in-country" rest and recuperation for the troops. By tacit agreement, almost no fighting took place there. Many were the tales of an American G.I. and a Viet Cong guerilla sitting side-by-side at a bar toasting this, that, and the other thing. My attitude was, "If I've got to be in Vietnam, Vung Tau is the place I want to be."

The living accommodations for the Navy contingent were relatively pleasant, at least by the standards of Vietnam. We were quartered in what had once been a motel, two men to a room with basic beds, bureaus, desks, chairs, and (wonder of wonders!) working lavatories. The buildings were situated on approximately two acres of land, surrounded by a chain-link fence on three sides and a vast swamp on the fourth. One man with an M-16 rifle guarded the single entrance, and there was always a pack of dogs hanging out at his feet. Several sandbagged bunkers were sited around the grounds for use in the event of an enemy attack, but we all knew that they were likely to be death traps—the timbers holding them up were riddled with termites (from inside the bunkers, one could hear the buzz of the termites at work) and the bunkers were at risk for imminent collapse even in the absence of explosions.

Lizards were everywhere—climbing the trees, scurrying along the ground, and hanging out on the walls and ceilings of our rooms. Most of them were in the range of 3 – 6 inches long, but there were several in the range of 18 – 24 inches long.

Water Monitor

One of the big ones resided right outside my room, and every morning at sunrise, it would make a crowing noise just like a rooster. Once I got used to them, I realized that it was nice having the lizards around because they significantly reduced the bug population. While I never saw one myself, I heard reports of a 6-foot lizard (presumably of the type variously known as "water monitor," or "water dragon") coming into our compound from out of the swamp and occasionally making off with one of our dogs.

I moved into what had been my predecessor's quarters. Strangely, nobody ever spoke of him, but I did find out that he was one of the few U.S. military people to be killed in Vung Tau—having been shot one evening while returning to the compound after visiting his mistress. It had been several weeks since he had been killed, but nobody had done anything with his personal effects—that was left up to me. When I opened the top drawer of what had been his bureau, a swarm of 2-inch long bugs (my lack of entomological knowledge left me at a loss relative to their identity) flew up into my face. I beat a hasty retreat, found some bug-killer spray, and emptied a couple of cans of the stuff into the bureau. When all was said and done, the "body-count" of the critters was in excess of 30.

One of the collateral duties to which I was assigned was that of Compound Defense Officer. I knew nothing about defending a compound, but then nobody else in our contingent probably did either—we were, after all, Navy, not Army—so I ended up being awarded "the honors." One

M-16 Rifle

of my responsibilities was to brief the "newbies" on the use of the M-16 rifle, about which I knew very little. During the very first checkout that I did, I managed to demonstrate my ineptitude for the job. After talking the man who I was "training" through the process of disassembling and reassembling the rifle, and stressing the importance of "safety first," I somehow managed to unwittingly chamber a cartridge and pull the trigger, putting a bullet through the ceiling of my room.

One evening, I was working at the desk in my room when I heard the sound of an automatic weapon firing within the compound. Throwing on my flak jacket and helmet and grabbing my rifle, I rushed out into the compound to find out what was happening. Our commanding officer was standing there holding a smoking M-16. As diplomatically as I was able, given my incredulity, I asked him what on earth he was doing. He told me that he had spotted a water monitor sneaking out of the swamp, and he had attempted to kill it. Well, he had been firing an M-16 in full automatic mode at a target not much smaller than a human being, and less than 50' feet away, yet he had managed to miss with every single round. I no longer felt quite so embarrassed at my own ineptitude with the M-16.

Another evening, there were several small explosions that seemed to have originated just outside the perimeter of our compound. Our commanding officer ordered me to take a patrol outside the compound perimeter to deal with whatever was going on. I thought this was unwise, given that none of us had the requisite training and hadn't the slightest idea what we were doing. Discretion being the better part of valor, I believed it was best that we stay inside the fence. Orders being orders, however, I did as I was told. Several enlisted men, who, unlike me, had actually volunteered for the task, and I straggled out onto the dirt road that ran along the front of the compound. While we were trying to figure out what on earth to do, a contingent of Army Military Police fortunately showed up and told us to get back inside the compound immediately. When nothing further happened and things had settled down, the senior Military Policeman demanded to know who had been dumb enough to lead a patrol outside the gate. Well, that was I, so I stepped forward, and he gave me a stern lecture about my "poor judgment," saying he would be writing up a report to that effect. My boss, our unit commander, was standing right there listening to all of this, and never once intimated that he had been responsible for giving me the order. I felt isolated, abandoned, scapegoated, and betrayed. So much for loyalty down the chain of command. Sure, he had a career to protect, but he was doing so at my expense.

~ ~ ~

The job of Coastal Surveillance Force watch officer seemed like it was almost custom-made for me. It involved lots of organizing and coordinating—two things I am very good at—and we performed our duties in a modern, comfortable, air-conditioned building at the top of a small mountain overlooking the South China

Swift Boat (PCF)

Sea. Each watch officer supervised a team of about 6 enlisted men, and there was sufficient downtime to allow for some camaraderie and bonding. We were essentially "guardian angels" for whatever "Swift Boats" (PCF or Fast Patrol Craft)

were operating at the time. We were there to help them out with communications and support—naval gunfire, artillery, air strikes, and Medevac helicopters—whenever needed. The boat crews depended on us and very much appreciated our assistance.

After I had been on the job for several weeks, some paperwork, originated by the Task Force Commodore in Cam Ranh Bay (my boss's boss), made the rounds inquiring as to who wanted to volunteer to go aboard the Swift Boats when they were undertaking "river-raider" operations in the "free-fire zones" of the Mekong Delta. A "free-fire zone" was an area that had been declared to contain no "friendlies"—that is, no allied troops, and no innocent civilians. All the inhabitants had been told to move out of the area, and that anyone who remained would be treated as the enemy. Anything that happened to someone who chose to remain in, or return to, a free fire zone would be their own fault. The designation of "free-fire zone" meant that American troops were essentially authorized, even encouraged, to kill anything that moved within them. In a free-fire zone, a high body count could be pursued without the encumbrance of needing to differentiate between combatants and civilians. This gave rise to the saying, "If it's Vietnamese, and if it's dead, then it's Viet Cong." In the military, a request for volunteers is tantamount to an implied order. I, however, chose to take the "request" at face value and opted not to volunteer. All of the other watch officers did volunteer, but I considered volunteering to be what one does when one actively wants to do something. Increasing the risk to life and limb was not something I actively chose to do and, in my judgment, it wasn't necessary for me to go on those raids in order to do my job properly. Not surprisingly, the Task Force Commodore didn't see it my way.

I was called on the carpet in his office. After flying the 200 miles to Cam Ranh Bay, I eventually entered the Commodore's office where I had to stand at attention while he berated me. In a lengthy tirade laced with multiple expletives, he told me that he didn't want in his command "a god-damned yellow-bellied, pinko, peacenik, especially some son-of-a-bitch who refuses to obey orders." He stated that he had at least three different counts on which he could court-martial me, and that, by God, he was going to make at least one of them stick. When he was done, I quietly requested permission to speak, and to level with him. That set him off again and he told me that I had damned well better level with him, or he would find some additional basis on which to court-martial me. I raised the volume of my voice to match his, used vocabulary similar to his (but somewhat toned down in deference to his rank), and stated clearly that while I was not a career naval officer, I was not "a yellow-bellied, pinko, peacenick," and that the question of disobedience of orders was irrelevant since his initial communication had been framed as "a request for volunteers." I also asserted that I was fully prepared to obey any appropriate and lawful order. He questioned my competence to determine what orders were "appropriate and lawful," to which I responded that it was ultimately a moral judgment on my part, and had nothing to do with my "competence" as judged by others. I also stated that I believed a specific direct order to go on the raids, given to me, and me alone, would be petty and vindictive—and that, on principle,

I would probably fight him on that, to the detriment of both of us. We continued yelling at each other for an extended period of time. Unexpectedly, he then lowered his voice and said, "Lieutenant Ritchey, I've decided not to court-marital you, and I think I will raise some of the marks on your fitness report. You are dismissed." That was it. Filled with incredulity, I flew back to Vung Tau. None of the other watch officers, who had, in fact, volunteered to do so, were ever sent on the raids. I assumed this was because the original "request for volunteers" was nothing more than a "testing of the waters."

~ ~ ~

In June of 1969, Special Forces operatives surreptitiously executed Thai Khac Chuyen, a suspected double agent. Seven of the men involved, as well as Colonel Robert Rheault, the commander of all Special Forces troops in Vietnam, were arrested and charged with premeditated murder—this despite the fact that they were doing exactly what they had been trained to do, and despite their having sought CIA approval before taking action. This incident, which became known as the "Green Beret Affair," caused considerable cynicism and outrage among the Special Forces troops and the American public, who believed that the Army had scapegoated those who had been arrested. The CIA, citing national security issues, refused to make its personnel available for testifying at a court martial, and, in September of 1969, President Nixon quashed the charges. The fact was not lost on me that, had I not insisted on my withdrawal from the black intelligence school at Fort Holabird, I could have ended up in a position similar to that of those soldiers.

Some weeks later, my boss told me that our operations officer (the man who supervises and coordinates the work of the watch officers and who plans the operations for the boats) was leaving soon, and that he wanted me to take on that job. That was fine by me—it gave me more command authority and responsibility, as well as the opportunity to learn a great deal more. The supervising and coordinating part of the job was easy—it was simply a matter of broadening the scope of what I had already been doing, researching extensively so as to develop an understanding of why things were done the way they were done, and looking for ways to improve our procedures. Planning the operations for the boats was more of a challenge because it was something I had not done before.

Along the way, of course, I made some mistakes, and there is one that still haunts me. It had to do with the way we handled medical evacuations ("Medevacs"). Normally, when one of our men on the boats was wounded, it was our job to arrange for a Medevac helicopter to pick him up and bring him to the hospital. Historically we had relied on an Army medical evacuation team in Vung Tau—and since they were Army, their working with us was a matter of informal personal agreements rather than official policy. Official policy was that we were to use a Navy medical evacuation team out of Can Tho on the Mekong River, some 80 miles to the Southwest. That seemed to make sense because both medevac teams were about the same distance away from our primary areas of operation and, since using the Navy unit was in accordance with policy, we should have more in the way of official support for our Medevac requests. I therefore entered in the watch officers' logbook that we were henceforth to use the Navy team from Can Tho.

Shortly thereafter, one of the men on the boats was seriously wounded and the watch officer dutifully called the Navy Medevac team in Can Tho. We had all gotten used to a 20 – 30 minute response time from the Army team in Vung Tau. After 40 minutes, everybody started to get worried. The watch officer again called Can Tho and was told that the Medevac helicopter was "on its way." The clock continued to tick and it wasn't until 90 minutes after the first call that the helicopter arrived.

Medevac Helicopter

By that time, the wounded sailor had died. Everybody involved was quite upset, and much of their anger was understandably directed toward me. I was probably more upset than just about anybody, because I held myself personally responsible for the man's death. Yes, the instructions I had given to the watch officers were in accordance with official policy, but I had ignored the dictum, "If it ain't broke, don't fix it." It was a painful way to learn the lesson that, in Vietnam, the way to get the job done was to ignore official policy and to go with "what works." We went back to using the Army Medevac team in Vung Tau.

It took some doing for me to learn how to plan "river-raider" operations. To begin with, we were working with the wrong boats. We had a fleet of Swift Boats (PCF or Fast Patrol Craft) and a couple of Coast Guard Cutters (WPBs) that had originally been intended for close inshore work—the interdiction (known as

"Operation Market Time") of ocean-going vessels trying to smuggle arms and such into South Vietnam. The Coastal Surveillance Force had done its job very well, and the enemy had given up trying to resupply in that manner. This created something of a vacuum—lots of boats with nothing to do—so the patrol areas of the Swift Boats were shifted to the lower reaches of the major rivers, thus freeing up the River Patrol Boats (PBRs) to move further upriver. Our basic patrol work on the major rivers went fine, but when it came to raids into the small canals of the free-fire zones, the boats were just too big. The River Patrol Boats that had previously shouldered this responsibility were 32' long with a beam of 11' and a draft of 2'. The Swift Boats were 50' long with a beam of 13' and a draft of 4', and the WPB behemoths were 82' long with a beam of 18' and a draft of 6'. Consequently, we could only schedule raids during periods of high tide, and the enemy could therefore easily predict, usually to within the hour, when our boats would be coming. At the anticipated time of a raid, most of the enemy would go into hiding and a couple of small Viet Cong teams with rocket-propelled grenades would position themselves where they could take quite a toll on our boats. It was definitely not a good set-up, but it was what I had to work with. I tried to come up with some creative solutions, but doubt that I was particularly successful.

One thing I became obsessed with was intelligence reports of American prisoners of war in our area of operations. Most of the reports were hoaxes or the result of over-active imaginations, but if even one of the reports were factually accurate, I wanted to do everything humanly possible to effect a rescue. I found myself continually obsessing about the unspeakable horrors that those poor Americans must be experiencing. Whenever I had the time, I would study the intelligence reports, plot the positions on a map, and try to think of effective rescue strategies. Nothing came of my efforts, and to this day, the possible fate of those unfortunate men, if there really were any, continues to haunt me.

Since I was responsible for planning the raids, it was obvious that I needed to go along on some of them so that I knew, first-hand, exactly what my people were up against. The first raid that I went on was into a relatively large canal in one of the free-fire zones. Predictably, one of the teams of Viet Cong with rocket-propelled grenades greeted us in a not-so-friendly fashion, and scored a hit on one of our boats. I was operating in

an observing, rather than a commanding, role, and I was stationed with an M-79

M-79 Grenade Launcher

grenade launcher, in the wheelhouse of the boat I was riding. I fired multiple rounds and, at some point, was nicked on the finger by some shrapnel. While my wound wasn't serious, it did bleed a lot. Prior to my becoming aware of the blood, I had apparently wiped the sweat from my brow with my injured hand, and blood was streaming down my face. The boat captain thought that I had suffered a head wound, and became very concerned, but we quickly figured out what the reality of the situation was, and carried on with our business. Another couple of days elapsed before we completed our patrol. We ran out of drinking water because a bullet had punctured the water tank, and all we had to drink for the rest of the patrol was pineapple juice, at the ambient jungle temperature of about 90 degrees. To this day, I find pineapple juice, and anything having to do with pineapples, to be absolutely abhorrent.

When I returned to Vung Tau, the "wound" on my finger had become infected and required medical attention. My boss told me to write myself up for a Purple Heart medal. I declined, stating that the wound was minor, that it was probably as a result of my own ineptitude with the M-79 grenade launcher (I had received no training whatsoever in its use), and that I didn't want to trivialize the awarding of a purple heart. He said that he was giving me a direct order to write myself up for that medal, the implication being that I could be court martialed for disobeying a direct order. I still declined, and he eventually let it go. One might wonder why he had such an investment in my receiving the Purple Heart. Well, that was the way it was with medals in Vietnam. A commanding officer's fitness report was based on many things, one of which was the number of medals received by the men under his command. The more medals, the better his fitness report.

Purple Heart Medal

Vietnam Service Medal

Illustrative of the plethora of medals awarded is the case of the Vietnam Service Medal. Essentially, everybody got one. All that was required for eligibility was that the service member have served anywhere in the Vietnam theater of operations for one or more days. The criteria were so loose, that we called it "The I Was Alive In '65 Medal." While I am unable to locate any specific data on the number of such medals awarded, it was presumably in excess of three million. The ribbon associated with the Vietnam Service Medal appears on the back cover of this book.

~ ~ ~

Much that occurred for me in Vietnam had a Kafkaesque quality to it. "Kafkaesque" is a word describing a nightmarish situation, which has surrealistic qualities, and is often dangerous, yet which most people can somehow relate to. Most of my experiences of this sort were in the interpersonal, rather than the physical realm, but one such experience in the physical realm that especially stands out in my mind did occur when I was safely ashore in Vung Tau. Several of the officers were going out to dinner at a fancy French restaurant, and invited me to go along. I explained that I couldn't go because I had a river-raider operation planned for that evening, and needed to be available to the watch officer on duty in case something went wrong. They suggested that I bring along a portable radio so I could be in constant contact with the watch officer at the Coastal Surveillance Center. That seemed like a workable solution, so off we went with me lugging along the radio. The restaurant was lovely. It was located high up on a hillside, and was very French in character. We were seated outdoors on a delightful patio filled with gorgeous tropical flowers, and offering a breathtaking view of the ocean. Shortly after we settled in with our wine, pate de foie gras, and caviar, a brilliant light show made its debut in the sky to the Southwest of us. While it was too far away for us to hear the associated sounds, I recognized from its location that our boats must be in contact with the enemy. For the next hour and a half, we indulged ourselves in gourmet wining and dining, while I monitored the progress of the firefight on my radio. It was an experience that would have fit well into the movie, *Apocalypse Now*. Of all the movies produced about Vietnam, that was the one I can most relate to despite, or perhaps because of, it's being the most surreal of the bunch.

~ ~ ~

The canals into which we conducted our river-raider operations were located in an area that had been designated as a "free-fire zone," and were therefore a great place to rack up body counts. Body counts were what the war in Vietnam Nam was all about. We weren't fighting a territorial war in which the objective was to capture and hold land, we were fighting a war of attrition in which the objective was to kill enough enemy soldiers that the enemy would run out of manpower and would eventually have to capitulate.

Body counts were especially important to the individual senior commanding officers because they were another element on which their fitness reports were based. Free-fire zones were designated as such by "standing orders" which "everybody knew about," yet I never once heard, or saw in writing, a direct order as to how they were to be dealt with. The belief that the people had been warned, given a chance to get out, and made their choice to remain, served as the basis for our forces rationalizing away the moral issues involved.

There were also very complex legal issues relative to free-fire zones that had to do with international law. The Geneva Conventions set the standards for humanitarian treatment of the victims of war. Grave breaches of the Conventions, such as the willful killing of unarmed civilians, are considered to be war crimes and are punishable as such. The Nuremberg Principles state that the fact that an individual committed such a war crime, while acting pursuant to the orders of his government or of a superior does not relieve him from responsibility under international law, provided a moral choice is in fact available to him. Free-fire zones, as defined, are a severe violation of the international laws of war. First, they violate the rule against willful attacks on civilians by presuming that any and all people remaining in such an area are enemy combatants and may therefore be lawfully attacked. Second, they violate the rule against indiscriminate attack by presuming that warning civilians to leave eliminates the requirements to discriminate in the targeting of weapons. Clearly, an order to "kill anything that moves" in a free-fire zone is in direct violation of international law and, as such, is an "unlawful order." Such an unlawful order presents a legal dilemma from which there is no escape. On the one hand, if an individual refuses to obey such an unlawful order, he faces the possibility of legal punishment at the national level for refusing to obey orders. On the other hand, if an individual accepts, and acts upon, such unlawful orders, he faces the possibility of legal punishment at the international level. This is a quintessential Catch-22, and is presumably the reason that senior officers refrained from giving direct orders about how those doing the fighting were to conduct themselves in a free fire zone. It provided them with "plausible denial" in the event issues of international law were to come into play. They could lay off all responsibility on the junior officers and the troops on the ground. This was a prime example illustrating the saying that, in the military, "Shit flows downhill."

Not surprisingly, the day eventually came when I had to deal with this dilemma head-on. Our boats were on a raid into a free-fire zone when they came across a village in which there were about 30 old men, women, and children. The raid commander called me on the radio to inquire if I intended to give them a direct order to kill everybody. Thankfully, I had already given this issue a lot of thought, and had decided my choice needed to be made on a moral, not a legal basis. Legal niceties be damned! I ordered them not to fire, but to take a few prisoners for interrogation, to propagandize the rest, and then let them go with a warning. I was very much concerned about the potential legal fall-out for myself, but at least my conscience was clear.

The repercussions were quick in coming. Again, I was ordered by the Task Force Commodore to appear in his office in Cam Ranh Bay the next day; again, I had to stand at attention while he shouted at me employing any number of choice epithets; again, I requested permission to level with him and to speak my own truth; again, he ordered me to do so. Although I was tempted, I thought it unwise to tell him of my belief that his anger arose primarily out of my depriving him of additional body count; I also thought it unwise to ask him to issue direct orders, in writing, about how we were to conduct ourselves in a free-fire zone. Instead, I spoke to him of the Geneva Conventions, of the Nuremberg Principles, of the legal Catch-22, and of the moral principles involved. Much to my surprise, he listened to me carefully, told me that he was not going to court martial me, that I was clearly "a thinking man with a good head on his shoulders," and that I could do good work in the right job—but that job was not in a direct combat role, and was certainly not one where I would continue to be under his command. He dismissed me and told me to expect new orders.

I returned to Vung Tau and, sure enough, the orders arrived the next day. I was being sent as a liaison officer to the primary base of the River Patrol Force located in Can Tho on the Mekong River. I couldn't believe my good luck! This would be a relatively cushy job in a relatively safe location. If this were to be the only disciplinary action I would receive as a result of my following my conscience rather than "getting with the system," I knew I ought to count my blessings. I packed my gear, and prepared to set off for Can Tho the next day.

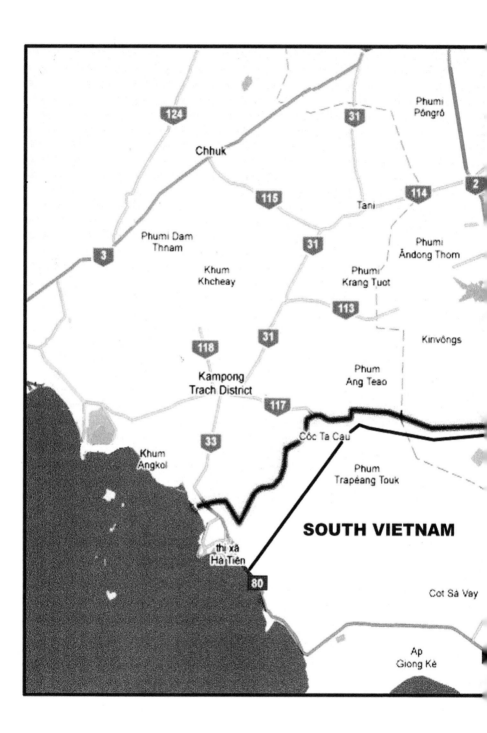

SOUTH VIETNAM

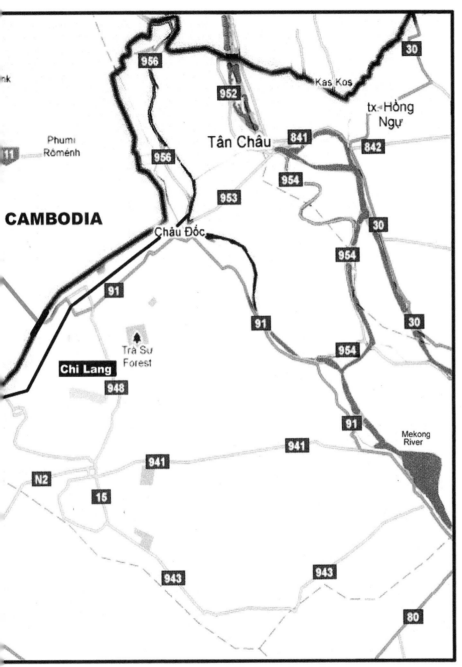

Map of area around Chi Lang, South Vietnam

31

CHAPTER 3
CHI LANG
(SEPTEMBER 1969 – NOVEMBER 1969)

I should have known better than to prematurely revel in my good fortune. In my experience, pleasant surprises seldom happened in the military. When I reported for duty at Can Tho, I was told that my orders had been changed, and that I was being sent to Chi Lang as Officer in Charge of the Naval Liaison Element to the Special Forces advisory unit stationed there. This job was much more like the disciplinary action that I had anticipated. The conditions would be primitive, and the situation would be as hazardous as any naval officer in Vietnam without specialized training might be exposed to. Once again, I felt betrayed—not so much because of the discipline, but because of the deception that was employed in the meting out of that discipline. I packed my bags again, and the next day set off for my new assignment.

Chi Lang was a God-forsaken little place about 60 miles Northwest of Can Tho and less than 10 miles from the Cambodian border. It was a gigantic sand pile surrounded on three sides by rice paddies, and backed up on the fourth by a cluster of small mountains. The locals were all said to be Viet Cong, and the mountains were reputed to be crawling with North Vietnamese Army troops. The only way in or out of the place was by airplane or helicopter, and each one of them managed to kick up a small sandstorm on arrival or departure. The temperatures during the day were in the 100 - 110 degree range, but were delightfully cool at night and made for good sleeping, if one could learn to tune out the incessant booming of artillery and the roaring of aircraft. We slept in large 12-person tents on cots positioned so as to avoid the trickles of water constantly entering from holes in the roof. We had no toilets, but we had a great six-holer outhouse. Showers were available using water that had been trucked in from a local stream and pumped up to an elevated storage tank with faucets piped off from it. The water was frigid, and one quickly learned to shower after 5:00 PM when the daylight sun had warmed up the water a bit, but before 7:00 PM when the coming of nightfall increased the likelihood of an enemy attack. Many a "newbie" had discovered the horrors of being naked and covered with soap when a rocket/mortar attack began.

The compound was relatively clean, but it did have a significant rat problem that was ameliorated by the South Vietnamese advisees who set numerous traps, caught the rats, and ate them. Our own food was surprisingly good, considering. Some of it was flown in, but most of it was purchased off the local economy, and that meant that it had to be soaked in a Clorox solution to kill all the bacteria resulting from the nature of the local "fertilizer." The Vietnamese women who helped in the kitchen thought this was unnecessary, and seldom bothered to inform anyone when the supply of Clorox was running low. I also heard that they saw no reason to go to the outhouse when they could squat right there on the slatted kitchen floor to relieve themselves. I was always amazed when another day went by and I hadn't contracted "Ho Chi Minh's Revenge."

Having arrived late in the afternoon, I decided I could wait until the next day before beginning to learn my new job, and meanwhile set about learning the ropes of living in that camp. I was told about the showers, advised where to locate my cot so as to avoid the rain, showed how to stow my clothes so they wouldn't become infested with bugs, and strongly advised to keep my mosquito netting tucked in tightly at night— not so much for protection against the bugs, but for protection against the rats. I inquired as to how it was possible to sleep with the constant booming of artillery, and was told that I would soon become so tired that the sound would seem to be little more than white noise. I also asked how I would be able to distinguish between the explosive sounds of "outgoing," and the explosive sounds of "incoming." The response was an enigmatic, "Oh, you'll know, you'll know." The first night, I lay there for a couple of hours thinking I would never be able to learn how to tune out the sounds of the outgoing artillery, but eventually I drifted off. Shortly thereafter, there was a new sound—this, a most unsettling whine that preceded an explosion. I knew instantly that this was the sound of incoming ordnance, and threw myself off the cot onto the floor, completely forgetting about the mosquito netting that I had so carefully tucked in before going to sleep. I became completely entangled and, by the time I freed myself and got all of my clothing and gear together, the attack was over. From that night on, I decided to take my chances with the rats—I got rid of the mosquito netting, slept in full uniform with boots on, and kept my flak jacket, helmet, and rifle close at hand.

~ ~ ~

The predicted fatigue soon set in. I was working at least 18 hours a day, and the time left over for sleeping was often interrupted by enemy attacks. We experienced rocket/mortar attacks about every third night. They were so frequent that they became almost routine. Ground attacks were a different story. Ground attacks occurred about once every two weeks and the "pucker factor" was always very high. One night, several weeks after I arrived, we were subjected to a major ground attack that lasted 6 hours—estimates were that at least 500 enemy were involved. They came down off the mountains, and attacked our camp from a large open field to the West, using multiple drainage ravines to provide themselves with cover. Fortuitously, a company of South Vietnamese Army soldiers had been positioned in that field the day before, and their presence provided us with much needed advance warning. The enemy was very aggressive, and our situation became quite precarious for a time. We radioed just about everyone, everywhere, for all the assistance we could get.

After a couple of hours in the bunkers, we eventually came out into the open to watch the show. The noise was deafening, but the visuals were good enough to put any Independence Day celebration back home to shame. My way of dealing with the chaos and the terror was to completely detach from it, and I even toyed with the idea of launching into song about

Puff, The Magic Dragon

"the rockets' red glare, the bombs bursting in air." The pyrotechnics were incredible—intense white light from flares, explosions from bombs, rockets, and mortars everywhere, and a seemingly infinite number of streaks of yellow light given off by tracer rounds fired from automatic weapons. There was also the addition of something new, different, and truly impressive, that I had never seen before. This was what was spoken of as "Puff, The Magic Dragon." It was a Douglas AC-47 (a converted DC-3 cargo plane) that was capable of firing 18,000 rounds per minute, and could put a bullet in every square yard of a football field in 20 seconds. The rounds came so fast, that they didn't sound like weapons firing at all, but rather like a very loud chain saw. The tracer bullets laid down a very beautiful and very reassuring carpet of gold.

At one point, I found myself absolutely entranced by a twisting, turning, seemingly alive, red, and purple fireball that was created by the explosion of an incoming rocket. I was startled out of my reverie when there was a loud "whump" on the ground a few feet away from me. Somebody yelled "grenade" and I dove for cover in the bunker. My blood ran cold, and I felt like I wasn't able to breathe, but nothing further happened and, after a few moments, I came out of the bunker and started exploring. I found a hot piece of rocket shrapnel, about 3" by 1," on the ground, and was completely unable to figure out how it traveled from the source of the explosion to where it landed on the ground without passing through my body.

As dawn approached, a detachment of United States armored cavalry appeared on the horizon. With flags flying, and kicking up large clouds of dust, they raced to our rescue. It's probably just my imagination in retrospect, but I'm inclined to believe that somewhere, somebody was playing "charge" on the bugle. In any event, we all heaved a sigh of relief when we realized that we were going to be okay.

After daybreak, things settled down and we were able to assess the situation. Thirty-six enemy soldiers had penetrated our perimeter, and all had been killed. Going out into the field, we found one South Vietnamese soldier who had dug his foxhole near the end of a drainage ravine that came very close to our compound perimeter. Whenever an enemy soldier came up out of the ditch, the soldier was able to dispense with him with a single round from his rifle. The bodies of at least 12 North Vietnamese Army troops surrounded him, and he received many accolades.

~ ~ ~

Learning my job at Chi Lang was a relatively easy matter. While the terrain, the cast of characters, and the boats were all different from what I had dealt with in Vung Tau, my responsibilities were still basically the same—planning operations for the boats, and providing them with whatever support they needed. This time, they were River Patrol Boats (PBRs) operating

River Patrol Boat (PBR)

primarily on a canal that ran for some 40 miles along the Cambodian border. The biggest difference in the jobs was that I needed to work very closely with the U.S. Special Forces and, through them, with the South Vietnamese military, in all its various forms. In retrospect, I find myself incredulous that the Navy would have put me, a 26-year-old "kid," in a position with that much independent authority, and responsibility for scores of lives. Naive, inexperienced young men can effectively carry out the orders they are given. But requiring one of them, essentially unsupervised, to work his own way through the Byzantine dynamics of the situation and then issue orders that put scores of lives at risk, seems to have been the height of folly.

The Lieutenant Colonel who commanded the U.S. Special Forces advisory unit was great! He was fair, realistic, reasonable, apolitical, and loyal to his men. These qualities were not necessarily appreciated by the "big brass," but they endeared him to all of us who worked closely with him. In my opinion, he was one of the best military officers I had ever met. He was, however, perhaps not well suited for a command in South Vietnam. This because he was totally oriented toward what he considered to be the mission, followed the dictates of his conscience, and gave no thought to political exigencies. He had resigned himself to the likelihood of never being promoted to full colonel, and suspected he might be involuntarily relieved of his command at any time.

The U.S. Special Forces intelligence officer was a most memorable character. Blond haired, blue eyed, standing 6' 4" tall, and weighing 250 pounds, all of it muscle, he had been born in East Prussia, and had served in Hitler's Youth Corps during the Second World War. He had been captured by the Russians, escaped, made his way to West Berlin, and returned to East Germany as an agent for the U.S. Army. Later he transferred to Korea where he was stationed for a number of years, and eventually wound up in Vietnam where he had been for almost a decade. He was absolutely fearless and he loved his work. He thought nothing of putting on camouflage paint at night, slipping out under the perimeter wire completely alone, entering the local village, capturing a suspected Viet Cong, and bringing him back to the camp for interrogation. While his interrogation techniques would be utterly abhorrent to almost anybody, they were less so to those of us who depended on him for our safety. His methods were generally successful, and the information they revealed saved us from dangerous enemy surprises any number of times. Shortly after I arrived at Chi Lang, he took me aside, and told me that it was clear that I was as green as they come, that I had no idea how to do what Special Forces troops had to do, and that when—that is *when*, not *if*—the camp was overrun, my chances of survival were minimal. He told me that when the overrun happened, I was to locate him, attach myself to him like glue, and he would get me out safely.

Another memorable character was a young Air Force pilot who regularly invited me to go with him in his little single-engine, propeller-driven, spotter plane for "joy rides" over the major North Vietnamese Army base just across the Cambodian border from us. Although it wasn't necessary for my job, and although violating Cambodian airspace was technically illegal, I eventually agreed to go along for the sake of camaraderie. Once was more than enough. I found no "joy" whatsoever in the large quantity of enemy weapons fire directed at our unarmed, defenseless little airplane. The only thing I learned was what it felt like to be one of those ducks in an amusement park shooting gallery.

Spotter Plane

The Navy Commander in charge of all of the area's River Patrol Boats (with whom, rather than for whom, I worked) was also great. His headquarters were on a cluster of barges in the Mekong River about 20 miles away from Chi Lang. He and I pretty much saw eye-to-eye, but his staff tended to ignore me, so every time it was imperative that I get something accomplished, I had to jump the chain of command, and go directly to him. He was okay with that, but it certainly didn't win me any friends among his staff.

I'm not sure what my predecessor had been doing, but from what I could tell, it didn't qualify as functioning in a liaison capacity. As was the case with my predecessor at Vung Tau, nobody ever spoke of him. I gathered that he had been transferred, not killed, but that was about it. He had never introduced the army commander and the navy commander to each other, despite their being only 20 miles apart by helicopter. Arranging that introduction was one of the first items on my agenda. The two commanders became fast friends, and did a lot to help each other out in tight situations. They even went so far, from time to time, as to put their own forces under each other's temporary command. While inter-service rivalries were a serious problem in many areas of Vietnam, they didn't exist in our little corner of the country—perhaps because we were truly dependent on each other for survival. In any event, it soon became clear that I was the only person in the area who knew what both the Army and the Navy were up to, so whenever one needed support from the other, it was up to me to make that happen.

One of the best aspects of my job was that I was essentially a free agent—my nominal "boss," 60 miles away in Can Tho, hardly knew I existed, and didn't really care—so I could act quite independently and do what I thought was right without having to take into account anybody else's agenda. The downside of that was that I had nobody to turn to for advice, guidance, and support, so I felt isolated and alone, completely alone. Just about every day I had to deal with "the big brass," both Navy and Army, in what essentially amounted to a consulting capacity. Other than calling them "sir," I felt it was my job to address them as equals so that I could tell them what I felt they needed to hear, rather than trying to figure out what it was that they wanted to hear from an underling. The Commander of Naval Forces Vietnam flew in from Saigon to visit me a couple of times, and whenever I told him of the problems we were encountering, he would just give me a pep talk. I knew that I was supposed to pretend that everything was "hunky-dory," and that such problems should never be put in writing, because then they could not be ignored. Contrarian that I am, I chose to put just about everything in writing, because I felt that transparency was vitally important. My superior officers were not pleased—but what were they going to do? Send me to Vietnam?

~ ~ ~

I experienced a great deal of anger, frustration, and disillusionment when I was confronted, first hand, with the corruption that ran rampant among our South Vietnamese "allies"—both financial corruption and military corruption. It wasn't a case of just a few "bad apples,"—corruption was endemic to the entire power structure of the country. Politicians and military officers, who were one and the same at higher levels, engaged in corruption on a regular basis, and were actually expected to do so. Financial corruption resulted in the loss of American dollars; military corruption resulted in the loss of American lives. It often seemed to me that my men and I were being sacrificed for the primary purpose of allowing the "fat cats" of South Vietnam to line the coffers of their Swiss bank accounts.

The motivations created by the "4Ps"—Power, Prestige, Position, and Pelf (money)—were very powerful. Anybody in a position of power, a province chief, for example, had to pay off his superiors in order to retain his job. He had to generate funds by graft, or he was summarily dismissed. There simply was no way for a man to remain truly honest and hold a high-level position. Even if he took no more than he needed, he still had to permit corruption to go on around him, and he had to embezzle money for the payoff demands made by his superiors. There was a long history of doing things this way in Southeast Asia, but in Vietnam, because of the war, the usual system of checks and balances had broken down, and it was a situation of every man for himself—and those in the higher echelons were becoming exceedingly wealthy.

Within this system, it appeared that all of the bigwig Vietnamese, everybody except the "little guy," was happy. Those in power were always dreaming up novel ways to acquire more money, and the peasant never knew when somebody would take away an even larger portion of his income. On paper, it might have appeared that the "government's" rate of taxation was reasonable, perhaps even less than the Viet Cong would demand (or were concurrently demanding), but in reality, the "government's" take was astronomical. Even this might have been tolerable if it were authorized and if it were stable, but it was not acceptable when the peasant's rate of taxation was subject to the whims and vagaries of every two-bit politician who happened to notice that he existed.

It seemed to me that we clearly weren't fighting "for democracy," but rather that we were fighting "against communism." Democracy simply didn't exist, and perhaps couldn't exist, in that country. Heretically, I believed that the general populace of South Vietnam would have been better off under communism. While a communist regime might have been harsh and totalitarian, the peasant would at least have had some idea of what to expect. I doubt that the little guy really cared much about such things as voting, freedom of speech, freedom of the press, etc. I thought that if he were given a relatively stable government and were left alone to tend to his crops, he would have been reasonably content.

~ ~ ~

Financial corruption and military corruption generally went hand in hand. One instance that directly affected me is particularly illustrative. Shortly after we had experienced a major ground attack in Chi Lang, the U.S. Special Forces advisors, without accompanying South Vietnamese, discovered a very large cache of enemy weapons—a total of 14 helicopter loads—and had them flown back to our camp. The commanding officer of the South Vietnamese Special Forces unit claimed the right to dispose of them. The U.S. Special Forces commanding officer would have none of that. He knew that the U.S. government would pay the South Vietnamese commander a significant reward, that the South Vietnamese commander would turn the weapons over to the South Vietnamese province chief, that the South Vietnamese province chief would resell the weapons to the enemy, and that those weapons would come back into our camp, but not by way of helicopters. He ordered the destruction of the enemy weapons. By doing so, he violated official policy and put his career on the line, but all of us in the camp heaved a sigh of relief. The South Vietnamese Army Special Forces commander was furious, and stormed off shouting that he was going to demand a new advisor. Nothing ever came of it.

American efforts to initiate significant battles were almost always frustrated by the South Vietnamese military commanders. In many cases, those commanders had made deals with the enemy providing them with safe passage. Even when they hadn't done this, the South Vietnamese military commanders went out of their way to avoid direct confrontation with the enemy. Often, when the Americans detected enemy activity, even in a free-fire zone, the South Vietnamese commanding officer would refuse to give firing clearance, saying that he had troops operating in the area (which we knew he didn't) or that those who the Americans had seen were only "friendly fishermen," that is, "innocent civilians." When contact with the enemy actually was made, as soon as a few casualties were taken, the South Vietnamese would withdraw for "regrouping," and that was the end of it. When an American advisor would try to convince his counterpart to take more aggressive action, he was usually told, "You only advise, I command." Also, the South Vietnamese military officers would repeatedly state that their orders were to observe and report, not to interdict—this despite the orders to interdict that had been given to the American advisors.

Occasionally a protracted battle with a relatively large enemy force would occur and, with the approach of nightfall, it became time to set up blocking positions. The South Vietnamese military would usually set up their positions on three sides of the enemy while leaving the fourth side wide open. No amount of arguing from the American advisor could change the situation and, of course, by morning the enemy had all disappeared. The South Vietnamese military could then move right in and "take the objective" without a single shot being fired. Everyone was happy except, of course, the Americans. On paper, the objective had been successfully taken with a minimum of friendly casualties. This wasn't a war of territorial objectives, however; it was a war of attrition, and, in that, the South Vietnamese had failed miserably. Once the "objective" had been taken, the South Vietnamese troops would withdraw, and the enemy would return within a few days.

It is natural to assume that South Vietnamese military officers who acted in this manner were Viet Cong, Viet Cong sympathizers, or, at the very least, "on the take." It was actually part of a much bigger picture that was based in policies established at the highest levels. South Vietnamese commanding officers were often operating under secret orders to do whatever they had to do to minimize their casualties, and any significant contact with the enemy was sure to increase those casualties. Those who were responsible for carrying out the operations knew that if they took significant casualties ("kill ratios" be damned), they would, at the very least, be relieved of their command. When the enemy had a major strongpoint that was of strategic value to him, one that it was clear he would fight for rather than abandon, the situation became really ludicrous. The South Vietnamese would then play ostrich, and flatly refuse to admit to the enemy's presence. When presented by the Americans with intelligence reports, sightings, and even photographs, the reflexive response was, "I do not believe this; it is all a fabrication." The American advisors were, of course, helpless to do anything, because, as their South Vietnamese counterparts so frequently reminded them, they only advised, they didn't command.

At night, we and the South Vietnamese both set ambushes. The ambushes set by the South Vietnamese military were laughable. The team would cluster together, build a fire, turn on their transistor radios, and go to sleep. The enemy would just make a minor detour around them. Those set by the U.S. Navy PBRs (we weren't supposed to call them "ambushes," we were supposed to call them "waterborne guard posts") were quite a bit more effective. We set one tenth the number of ambushes set by the South Vietnamese military, but we made contact with the enemy five times as frequently. Our ambushes could have been even more effective, but we were seldom able to get South Vietnamese permission to set ambushes near what we knew to be major enemy infiltration routes. One time we did get permission to do so, provided we took along South Vietnamese troops to "ensure our safety." For five nights our boats sat in ambush, and didn't see so much as a lizard move, so we decided to pack it in. Several days later we decided to have another go at it. Knowing that we didn't need South Vietnamese troops "for our safety," we didn't request them, and we somehow "forgot" to inform the South Vietnamese military of our plans. Within a couple of hours after our boats had moved into position, they made contact with an estimated 60 North Vietnamese Army troops, and fought a very successful battle. Officially, we were castigated for not having properly communicated our plans to the South Vietnamese, but I'm certain that the American "brass" were secretly quite pleased, if for no other reason than the body count they were able to add to their records.

The instances of military corruption that I observed were far too numerous to specify, but there is one I can think of that was absolutely typical. One night, about 3:00 AM, during the hours of curfew, the senior American Special Forces advisor was up with a flight of helicopters over a free-fire zone. They spotted 20 – 30 sampans moving through the area, and called for firing clearance, but it was denied and they were told by the South Vietnamese that those were just "friendly fishermen" getting an early start on their day. Frustrated, the commander ordered the helicopters to move in close and low in the hope that they would draw fire from the sampans, and then be able to return it, even without clearance. That's exactly what happened, and the helicopters shot up about a dozen sampans with perhaps 50 men aboard, getting multiple secondary explosions. The next morning when troops were inserted, there were just a couple of destroyed sampans and only a few bodies, all of them "friendly fishermen." This was how the enemy operated. They had taken a few friendly fishermen along with them and, soon after being engaged by our helicopters, they removed most of the destroyed sampans and all of the bodies of their troops. The result of this engagement, of course, was the creation of confusion and hard feelings between the

Sampan

South Vietnamese and the Americans.

Another instance that saddened me deeply and angered me enormously occurred shortly after the major ground battle in which our camp was almost overrun. Because we were in trouble and needed assistance, a company or so of Cambodian mercenaries, commanded by American officers, was sent to help us out. After they arrived, they took up residence for a couple of days in order to be briefed by us, and to get the lay of the land.

As an aside, we Americans had a number of dogs in

our camp—the Army had about six and the Navy had one. The Navy dog was a real wimp, and never left the side of whoever was on watch at the time. While Darwin would assert that "wimpiness" does not contribute to survival, in this particular case, that trait saved her life. The morning after the Cambodians arrived, the Army dogs had all disappeared and only the Navy dog remained. We ultimately figured out that those animals, which we Americans had viewed as our canine companions, had been viewed by the Cambodians as culinary delights. Despite the cultural differences involved, I couldn't help but be furious.

B-52 Bomber

The primary mission of the Cambodian mercenaries was to take and clear the small mountain that had been used by the North Vietnamese army as the staging area for its attack on our camp. This mission had been attempted a few times before by less effective units, and had always failed because they made frontal assaults up a valley that was completely controlled by a dug-in enemy. This unit, however, was going to approach the mountain from the backside, and come down over the top. They would be heavily outnumbered, but they would be supported by massive artillery fire and air strikes, including prepping by B-52s bombers, and we thought their chances of success were pretty good.

Their route of approach to the mountain took them through a large "secure" orchard—secure because there were three "friendly" outposts in the immediate area. They let their guard down, and were taken under fire by enemy troops, suffering 60 men killed in action. When they finally took the orchard, they discovered that the enemy had been operating from concrete bunkers and heavily fortified trench lines, some of them within 100 yards of a so-called "friendly" outpost. Three of the men who were killed were American officers with whom I had become friends. We had been seriously betrayed by the South Vietnamese military. In addition to my sadness, I felt outrage, even entertaining fantasies of finding my own way to the outpost and personally killing its commanding officer. That not being such a good idea, my only option was to suppress my feelings. Nevertheless, I believed that the outpost's commanding officer should be shot as a Viet Cong, or at least as a Viet Cong sympathizer.

After my anger had subsided somewhat, however, I realized that the outpost commander really had no viable options. He had at his disposal no more than a platoon of soldiers, whereas the enemy forces were probably at least a company in size, so the "friendlies" were very much outnumbered. He knew that if he, or any other outpost commander, were to initiate contact, he would have to go it alone, because he would get no support from his superiors, and his outpost would likely be overrun. When all was said and done, other than the prepping of the mountain by the B-52 strikes, the assault on the mountain never happened.

I believed that one of the overriding problems with the South Vietnamese fighting capabilities had to do with the structure of their political/military establishment. It was highly centralized, and quite top-heavy. Subordinates were not permitted to take any action on their own initiative. Unit commanders were not permitted to request permission from, or make recommendations to their superiors. It was a matter of "face." All ideas—the entire concept of an operation—must appear to have sprung full-blown into some general's mind. Incredibly, if a junior officer were to take some initiative, and launch an operation on his own, he was liable to be sentenced to a long jail term at the very least, even if the operation were to succeed beyond anybody's wildest dreams. Such personal initiative was simply not permitted because the superior officers might end up losing face.

~ ~ ~

With each day that went by, my fatigue became more and more pronounced. I was self-medicating with 20 cups of coffee and 5 packs of cigarettes a day. When that proved to be insufficient, the army medic put me on an anti-depressant, a stimulant during the day, and a sedative at night. One morning I walked into the operations center and began what I thought would be a discussion with the U. S. Special Forces commanding officer about an upcoming operation. He stopped me and told me that I was speaking unintelligible gibberish. I tried again, believing that I was being quite clear, but the look of concern, confusion, and consternation on his face suggested otherwise. I was quite frustrated, but, amazingly, otherwise unconcerned. He sent me off to my cot, and told me to stay there until he sent for me. Clearly the fatigue and/or the medications were taking their toll, and I had crossed a line to where I now had significant medical/psychological problems. The army commander contacted my nominal boss in Can Tho who wasn't much interested, so he then contacted the commanding officer of the local River Patrol Boats. The navy commander helicoptered in to see me, and my speech was still pretty much incomprehensible. He said he would use the influence of his rank to see that I got sent off for previously scheduled rest and recuperation with my wife in Hawaii, and that I would then be transferred to a less arduous duty station when I returned to Vietnam. I stopped taking the medications, the use of which seems, in retrospect, to have been totally ill advised. They had, however, been prescribed by an Army medic, a presumed authority figure in whom I had put my faith and trust. I slept for a couple of days, not even having the energy to leave my cot during a rocket/mortar attack, and was soon on board a flight to Honolulu.

Going on R&R did provide the opportunity for *rest and recuperation*, but there was no opportunity for *relaxation and recreation*—both because of my physical/mental/emotional state, and because I came down with the worst strep throat I had ever experienced. Given that I was on R&R, I wasn't about to seek medical attention, and possibly end up being sent to some military hospital. My wife and I just hunkered down in our hotel room for the duration. When the week was over, I got aboard the plane back to Vietnam running a 103-degree fever. On the return flight, I passed out a couple of times, and was hospitalized right after I got off the plane in Saigon. A few days later, I was headed for my new duty station in Duc Hoa.

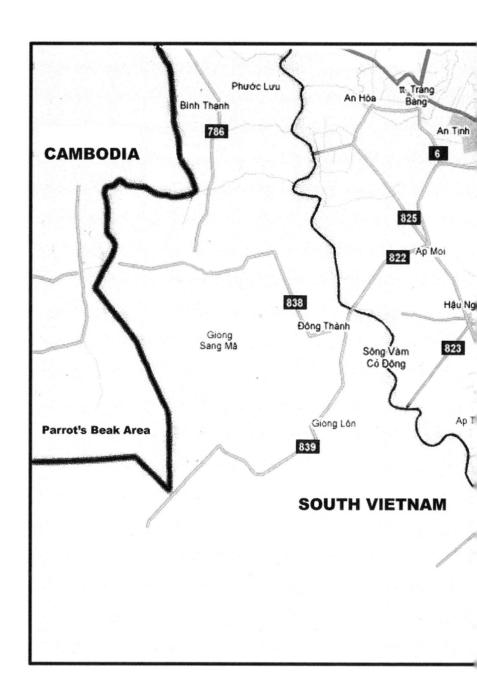

Map of area around Duc Hoa, South Vietnam

57

CHAPTER 4
DUC HOA
(NOVEMBER 1969 – MARCH 1970)

The base at Duc Hoa was a pretty big place, being the home of the 25th Infantry Division of the South Vietnamese Army, a notoriously corrupt and ineffective unit, even by Vietnamese standards. It was located 10 miles south of Cu Chi, home of the 25th U.S. Infantry Division, 15 miles west of Saigon, and 20 miles east of the "Parrot's Beak" area—so named for its appearance on a map—of Cambodia. As Officer in Charge of Naval Liaison Element, Duc Hoa, I was nominally attached to the U.S. Army advisors for the South Vietnamese 25th Infantry Division, but they thankfully ignored my existence and I was free to go about my business as I saw fit. My responsibilities were much the same as they had been in Chi Lang—providing support for the River Patrol Boats operating on the Vam Co Dong River approximately 10 miles from the Cambodian Border. The Commanding Officer of those PBRs, with whom I had little contact, was headquartered on a cluster of barges in the river approximately 30 miles to the South. My nominal boss was still the same unsupportive officer in Can Tho, and I had essentially no contact with him at all.

Once again, as was the case in both Vung Tau and Chi Lang, nobody ever spoke of my predecessor. I finally realized that it had nothing to do with the withholding of information, but was, rather, a function of the "easy come, easy go" syndrome. Since we were functioning as individuals, rather than as collective units, there was never any sense of cohesiveness. Each of us was nothing more than a replicable cog in the system, and as such, we were utterly disposable. It was impossible to form any long-term relationships that we could count on, and loneliness became a constant companion. While we might bond with each other for the short time we were together, our "buddies" of today might well be gone tomorrow—whether as a result of a casualty or a transfer—and, in order to protect ourselves psychologically, we had to adapt to the impermanence by adopting the attitude of "out of sight, out of mind." As a result, despite my having spent a year in Vietnam, I now only remember the name of one man I worked with, that being the Special Forces intelligence officer in Chi Lang, and that is only because he was one of the most memorable characters I have ever met.

Living conditions in Duc Hoa were relatively civilized. We slept in plywood barracks with screened windows, each of which held about 12 men with plenty of room to spare. The food was quite good and in plentiful supply. There was even an officers' club, of sorts, and things were sufficiently laid-back that I often went there to relax with a beer. Our sandbagged communications bunker, which was well air-conditioned for the radios, was set off by itself away from the army facilities, so I permitted my men to decorate it as they saw fit—which was, predictably, with a myriad of Playboy centerfolds. We had our own coffee pot, and there was even a cot where I could snooze if my watch-standers needed me to be immediately available.

~ ~ ~

A few weeks after I arrived in Duc Hoa, I learned that the Army medic who had prescribed the pharmaceuticals for me in Chi Lang had died of a self-administered overdose—whether accidental or intentional, I don't know. That news wasn't particularly surprising, but it was disturbing nevertheless, especially since the person who died could just as well have been me. Some time after that, I also learned that the Special Forces camp at Chi Lang had been overrun by the enemy. Again, while the news was disturbing, it wasn't particularly surprising. My breakdown turned out to have been a blessing in disguise because it got me out of Chi Lang just in time. I now wish that I had learned more about that incident—what happened, how it happened, who survived, and who didn't—but at the time, in order to protect myself psychologically, I chose to think of it as just one more instance of "easy come, easy go," and I just kept on keeping on.

There was a serious drug problem among the U. S. Army troops in Duc Hoa, and I was concerned about the possibility of my men getting caught up in it. I looked for ways to prevent that from happening and one of the ideas I came up with was to arrange for the Navy to have its own specified barracks with all of us bunking together. This was heresy as far as the Army was concerned—officers and enlisted men simply didn't bunk together—but I persevered and got my way. As far as I know, none of my men ever got involved in the drug scene.

It was a good thing that our camp was secure because the Army troops would often use drugs when they were on guard duty, and that might have severely compromised our safety if we were attacked. I refused to allow my men to be assigned to guard duty because they had enough to do with their primary responsibilities. Significant pressure was brought to bear on me personally, however, to join the rotation of officers in charge of the guard. I acceded so as to keep the Army happy, but it was an absurd situation because I didn't know the system, I didn't know the army troops, and they didn't know me. On my first night as officer in charge of the guard, I was making the rounds of the perimeter and found one guard who was smoking marijuana. I read him the riot act and told him to get rid of the joint. Later that same evening, as I made the rounds again, I came across that same soldier, this time sound asleep. I reprimanded him again, and told him that I was reporting him to the sergeant of the guard. As I was walking away, I heard the distinctive sound of an M-16 rifle being cocked. I looked over my shoulder and saw that he had his rifle pointed directly at me. My heart started racing and I broke out in a cold sweat, but all I could do was to keep walking, and duck around the corner of a building as soon as possible. I don't know what the consequences were for that soldier, but I never again had to be officer of the guard, presumably because I had been involved in a problematic situation.

Another step that I took to try to keep my men out of trouble was to institute "Sunday Morning Meetings." I managed to scrounge doughnuts, fruit, and such from the mess hall, and we all gathered at 9:00 AM in our communications bunker, wearing whatever informal clothing we chose, to talk about whatever was on our minds. I tried to introduce a subtle, non-intrusive element of spirituality into the meetings, and the men mostly wanted to raise questions about their circumstances—like "why are we here in Vietnam?" One theme that I regularly pursued was that of trying to set the record straight about what was really going on back home. The men had little information to draw on other than rumors and the biased reporting of the military newspaper, *Stars and Stripes*. My wife regularly sent me articles from various magazines and newspapers, so I was in a position to provide them with a more balanced perspective. Illustratively, the Stars and Stripes reporting on the "November War Moratorium" was an exercise in "yellow journalism." After the headline of "250,000 TURN OUT FOR PROTEST IN D.C." the article began with, "Shouting, paint-throwing extremists staged a wild demonstration at the Justice Department Saturday …" and then went on for many paragraphs describing the "yippies and other ultra-extremists" who were demonstrating against the government, against the military, and against the men who served in Vietnam. Drawing on the information I had available, I explained to my men that the vast majority of the demonstrators had behaved peacefully, that very few of them were "radicals" (in fact, many might have been described as "conservatives"), that they were primarily demonstrating against the war, not necessarily against the government or the military, per se, and they were definitely not demonstrating against the troops themselves (indeed, most were demonstrating in support of the troops and trying to get them out of an untenable situation). My explanations seemed to be useful in helping my men to put our circumstances into proper perspective.

One Sunday, during our meeting, an Army lieutenant colonel rushed in to announce that the Commander of Naval Forces Vietnam had just landed at the helicopter pad and was on his way over to see me. This was definitely "big brass" of the sort that the man wanted to impress, and he yelled at me to get my men in proper uniforms, remove the pinups from the walls, and do any number of other things so the Army wouldn't be embarrassed by having us in their presence. Through my rising irritation, as tactfully and respectfully as I was able, I reminded him that he was in a Navy facility that I commanded and for which he had no responsibility or authority, that it was a Navy officer who was coming to visit me, and that it was obviously an informal visit—otherwise I would have been informed in advance, and hence made the requisite preparations. I also told him that I would be sure to ask the Admiral not to hold the Army accountable for the way I was running my show. He was apoplectic, but he stormed out and left us alone. A few minutes later, the Admiral came in, took a look around, asked what we were up to, and, when I told him, said he was glad the men were getting an opportunity for relaxation and bonding, and would I mind if he took off his boots. He chatted with everybody, and the men thought he was great. In keeping with the policy of maintaining that everything was "hunky-dory," he sidestepped most of the problematic issues that I raised, but I was very thankful for his visit because it was a real morale-booster for my men.

Another thing that kept my men together and out of trouble was that they were always welcome in the communications bunker, which was delightfully air-conditioned to a temperature of 65 degrees, as was required for the radios. That, alone, was enough to get most of them to spend much of their free time there. One day the air conditioner stopped working and the bunker got very hot very quickly. Knowing that the radios would not last long in that heat, I sent off a message to all of the appropriate people requesting an immediate replacement for the air conditioner. The response I got was something to the effect that everybody wanted an air conditioner for all sorts of reasons, that the waiting list was a mile long, and that I could forget it. Given that the system often didn't work, we usually found ways to meet our logistical needs by calling in favors from our friends. Because air conditioners were in such sort supply, however, that approach was not effective in this case. With feelings of intense frustration, I sent off another message saying that we had four radios, and that after two of them went down, our unit would be going off-line so as to keep the remaining two radios in reserve for a true emergency. When the first radio went down after a day or so, I sent another message to the powers that be, informing them of that event and reminding them of what I would need to do when the second radio went down. I received no response. When the second radio went down after another day, I sent off another message saying that we were going off line and that we would be reachable only by telephone. The stark reality of the situation apparently caught somebody's attention, and we had a new air conditioner within 6 hours.

~ ~ ~

Over the months, I had sent any number of letters and messages to the "appropriate" people, attempting to have redressed what I considered to be the inequitable nature of my treatment, and to effect my earlier return home. All had been to no avail. Major troop withdrawals from Vietnam were occurring; 30 thousand of 35 thousand Navy personnel in Vietnam would be gone by July of 1970; many Navy officers were being discharged before their initial obligated service had been completed; the involuntary extension under which I was serving had been cancelled (or, to use the politically correct term, "more selectively applied"), yet I was still in Vietnam. I was regularly reminded that the "needs of the service" took precedence over the desires of the individual. Even though I assumed I would accomplish nothing, I continued to write letters because I had a lot of things I wanted to get off my chest. One lengthy letter that I sent to the Bureau of Naval Personnel had to do with what I perceived as the Navy's poor quality of personnel management, and was based primarily on my own experiences, which included:

- The cancellation of the extension of my assignment aboard the destroyer escort when my letter of resignation was received, and my subsequent orders to Vietnam coupled with an involuntary extension of my time in service. (See Chapter 1.)

- My being ordered to the "voluntary" Army black intelligence school and my being threatened with court martial when I declined to accept those orders. (See Chapter 1.)

- The lack of official Navy interest and assistance when I was having a breakdown in Chi Lang. (See Chapter 3.)

One personnel management situation that wasn't specifically about me, but which I felt to be particularly relevant was this: When one of my men was transferred elsewhere, I received as a replacement a Machinist's Mate first class who had given the Navy 18 years of excellent service with a pipe wrench and a sledge hammer. He was completely out of his element in a job where he had to use tact and diplomacy on the radio, plot positions on a map, and make life-and-death operational decisions. Not surprisingly, he quickly became a nervous wreck. I sent out a message requesting that he be transferred to a more suitable duty station and that I be sent another replacement. Receiving no reply, I sent him to the hospital for confirmation of my opinion about his psychological state. After receiving that confirmation, I sent off another message to which I received no reply. Ultimately I decided to force the issue and sent off a message to the effect that I was transferring him out, whether or not I got a replacement. I was told in no uncertain terms that my job was to make do with the people that I had, and that no replacement would be forthcoming. Extremely frustrated and worried about my man, I transferred him out anyway. Presumably because I had successfully called the Navy's bluff, I eventually got the replacement I needed.

I also wrote several letters to family and friends, politicians, and various news media, the basic theme of which was that we were fighting the wrong war in the wrong place at the wrong time, and that it was no wonder a large number of the American people were expressing their dissent. My basic points included the following:

- We had been fighting the war for a very long time (indeed, the longest war in our history), and we still had nothing in the way of tangible results to show for our efforts.

- We were fighting for an "ally" that had no commitment to winning the war, and whose leaders wanted to see the war extended indefinitely for the sake of their own personal gain.

- We were incurring the wrath of civilized (and not so civilized) nations around the world, and our national prestige was suffering.

- We could have won the war by now if we had fought it on our own terms, but we opted instead to fight it on the terms dictated by those in power in South Vietnam, and hence we were doomed to failure.

- Those who were demonstrating against the war were not necessarily radicals who wanted to bring down our government (despite the government's paranoia), but were, rather, sincere, committed citizens who wanted to bring our troops home.

- Senior officers were continually covering their tracks and, when anything went wrong, would blame it on the junior officers they used as scapegoats.

- The loyalty of the troops was not to the government or to the senior officers, who were not loyal to them, but was, rather, to their peers with whom they lived, worked, and died.

I doubt that I accomplished much of anything. I didn't really expect to, but I felt a responsibility to speak out, and I at least managed to get all of that off my chest.

~ ~ ~

On November 12, 1969, 20 months after the incident itself occurred, the story of the My Lai Massacre (we were supposed to call it an "Incident" rather than a "Massacre," but in my mind it was, and always will, be a massacre) broke in the Detroit News followed the next day by Seymour Hersh's reporting in the St. Louis Post Dispatch. A week later, CBS television began coverage, and Time, Life, and Newsweek magazines all picked up the story. The story was that on March 16, 1968, while on a search and destroy mission, Charlie Company, operating under the battalion-sized Task Force Barker of the Americal Division, entered the village of My Lai and other surrounding villages in an area that had been designated as a free-fire zone. Central to the events were the actions of Charlie Company's 1st platoon under the command of Lieutenant William Calley. They had expected to encounter fierce resistance, but that turned out not to be the case; all they found were old men, women and children, most, if not all, of whom were civilians—Viet Cong supporters, perhaps, but civilians nevertheless. Given that they were in a free-fire zone— which had been stressed by the company commander, Captain Ernest Medina, at the pre-operation briefing— and given that the standing orders for free-fire zones were to kill anything that moved, Lieutenant Calley ordered his men to open fire, and a mass slaughter ensued.

The incident was initially reported as a "fierce fire fight in which 128 Viet Cong were killed." Kudos were extended to Charlie Company from all levels of command, and senior officers rushed to ensure that the significant body count was added to their tally sheets. When the truth about "what really happened" began to see the light of day—ultimately the number of dead was estimated to be between 347 (United States estimate) and 504 (North Vietnamese estimate)—those same officers scrambled to cover their tracks and distance themselves from the whole thing. Disclaiming any personal responsibility for the incident, they began to look for junior officers they could scapegoat, and settled on Calley and, to a lesser extent, Medina. When all was said and done, only five men were court martialed, the ranking of them being Captain Medina, and only one, Calley, was convicted. Shortly after his conviction, Calley's sentence was commuted by President Nixon, presumably because of intense pressure from the American populace who expressed outrage over the obvious corruption and scapegoating involved.

That nobody up the chain of command knew what was going on, and nobody gave any orders that set the stage for the incident, was an absurd claim. The Army, however, used its directives as a shield to protect its honor and the reputations of the senior officers involved. During the court martials and various inquiries, the Army successfully prevented any examination of the relationship between the My Lai Massacre and such tactical concepts as "free fire zones," "search and destroy missions," "body count," and the behavior of Charlie Company.

Most of the soldiers were young (around 20 years old), away from home for the first time, not well educated, unaware of the legal niceties of such things as the Geneva Conventions and the Nuremberg Principles. They could hardly have been expected to make independent moral decisions under the pressure of orders and combat conditions. Calley was not much older than his men and not much better educated. Yes, they committed terrible acts of savagery, inexcusable acts, but the responsibility was never placed where it truly belonged—on the higher command levels of the Americal Division and on the "architects of policy," the people who had created the Vietnam strategy and who should have know where it would lead.

I have often thought how ironic it would have been if, while Calley and Medina were being court martialed for the massacre that was a direct consequence of their following standing orders, I were simultaneously being court martialed for *not* following those same standing orders when I was Operations Officer for the Coastal Surveillance Center in Vung Tau. I wrote to many of the "architects of policy" and to many of the news media, expressing my take on things, but nobody ever bothered to respond.

~ ~ ~

Duc Hoa and Cu Chi sat astride a major infiltration route from the Parrot's Beak area of Cambodia to Saigon, the distance between the two being only 35 miles. The Parrot's Beak was a major base and rest area for the North Vietnamese Army and the Vietcong, estimates being that some 40,000 to 60,000 enemy troops were located there. It was a major terminus point for the Ho Chi Minh trail down which thousands of troops and tens of thousands of tons of supplies regularly flowed from North Vietnam.

To counter the enemy threat, the United States and South Vietnam had positioned numerous large military units along the infiltration route, chief among them being the 25th Infantry Division of the United States Army (in Cu Chi) and the 25th Infantry Division of the South Vietnamese Army (in Duc Hoa). There were so many different military units operating in the area that they frequently got in each other's way and, of course, the political infighting and rivalries were extensive. Often, when we wanted to obtain firing clearance for our boats on the Vam Co Dong River, we would have to do so from as many as six different units. That was a time-consuming task and, by the time it was eventually completed, the enemy had usually disappeared, much to our chagrin.

One night we were kept waiting for an extremely long period of time while trying to get firing clearance from a South Vietnamese Army unit. As a result, a small group of Viet Cong had sufficient time to move into position, set up, and fire several rounds from a 75 mm recoilless rifle at one of our PBRs. They scored a hit and three U.S. sailors were killed. The senior Navy commander, responding in what had become his predictable manner, ordered the boats to the north and the south of the PBR that had been hit to move in and provide assistance. He also ordered that every aircraft in the vicinity converge to provide air cover, and told me to have the Army's artillery on call—all of this for an enemy force that probably consisted of no more than four men. Since that response was utterly predictable to me, it was also presumably predictable to the enemy, and they knew it left enormous gaps in our line of ambushes, which they could use to their advantage. Acting on instinct, I surreptitiously called one of my Air Force pilot friends and asked him to go up in his spotter plane over the Plain of Reeds, just south of the Parrot's Beak, and check to see what might be happening there. He spotted scores of sampans with hundreds of men on board, and was on the receiving end of much small-arms fire. Having been spotted, the enemy apparently assumed that air strikes and artillery would soon be targeted on them, so they turned around and headed back into Cambodia. They needn't have worried because the attention of all local American forces was focused on the PBR that had been hit—which, I assume, was exactly what the enemy had planned on.

Despite my being a relatively junior officer, I was included, to a certain extent, in the planning of the invasion of Cambodia (we were supposed to speak of it as a "campaign" rather than as an "invasion"). The brass included me, I presume, because I was on-site, and because I had first-hand experience of what both the Navy and the Army were doing. In retrospect, I find myself amazed, and also horrified, at the number of diabolical ideas I was able to come up with—but at the time, I was just doing my job. That invasion did, ultimately, occur during the months of April to July 1970. Multiple Navy units proceeded up the Mekong River to Prey Vang, Cambodia, thus permitting ground forces from the IV Corps in South Vietnam to move westward toward Phnom Penh.

One thing that was quite unusual about our Navy operations was that we were experimenting with the use of personnel sensors—acoustic, seismic, and magnetic devices—that had been placed by the Navy SEALS in the Plain of Reeds free-fire zone, just across the Vam Co Dong River. We regularly arranged for firing clearances in advance, so when the sensors were activated, we could respond almost immediately with artillery fire. Some time—generally 30 minutes to an hour—would usually elapse before we could get aircraft to the area to check out the results. Most often, signs of the enemy proved to be non-existent. Everybody was mystified. Eventually I suggested that the enemy might have a system of tunnels in the area in which they hid with their dead and wounded. I proposed that, instead of just sending observation aircraft, we send helicopters with troops that could be inserted to search for such tunnels. My suggestion was scoffed at, and I was told that, while there might be a tunnel or two in the area, nothing on the scale of what I was suggesting could possibly exist. Many years later, I came across a book entitled *The Tunnels of Cu Chi*. It spoke of the district of Cu Chi as being the most "bombed, shelled, gassed, defoliated, and generally devastated area in the history of warfare." It also stated that there were 30,000 miles of tunnels in North and South Vietnam, and that the tunnels were especially concentrated in the Cu Chi area with perhaps 100 miles of tunnels in the surrounding environs.

At the time, the existence of personnel sensors, in general, was a highly secret matter and information was not to be divulged to anyone without a definitive need to know. The way we handled this was by declaring the area around the sensors to be a "Restricted Zone," and by making it clear that no military units were to operate in that area without specific permission from us. In order to double up on our safety procedures, each morning we confirmed with all local military units that they would have no troops operating in that area for the next 24 hours. Everybody knew, from our calls for artillery and air strikes, that there were lots of enemy in that Restricted Zone. One U.S. Army Lieutenant Colonel, hoping to add to his body count, decided to insert some of his soldiers without asking our permission, which he probably believed would be denied. Not knowing of the existence of the sensors, he presumably figured he could get away with it. When the sensors were activated, we assumed it was caused by enemy troops, since that morning all friendly units had confirmed they would have no personnel in the area. We called for an artillery barrage, and ten U.S. soldiers were killed by "friendly fire" that I had initiated. Despite the incident's being a direct result of that officer's deceitfully circumventing safety procedures in an attempt at self-aggrandizement, I nevertheless held myself responsible for the deaths of those Americans. I was outraged and dismayed.

Over the next several days, I sent out numerous messages attempting to have him held accountable for his actions. He called me on the carpet and, flanked by two burly sergeants in his office, told me in a very matter of fact way that unless I ceased and desisted, he would arrange to have a couple of live fragmentation grenades rolled under my bunk one night while I slept. I did not doubt for a moment the reality of his intentions and, not wanting to add to the body count of dead Americans, I capitulated. In all honesty, I was terrified! This was clearly a situation in which I had everything to lose and nothing to gain by pursuing my point. As with so many other situations in Vietnam, since I had nobody to turn to for support, I just tried to forget about it. By that point in the war, "fragging" had become a relatively common event—indeed, some estimates hold that as many as one quarter of all American officers killed in Vietnam died under "suspicious circumstances." It was one way, albeit rather extreme, that the soldiers had of expressing their frustration and rage. I had never heard of a senior officer arranging to have a junior officer fragged, although I'm sure it occasionally happened.

~ ~ ~

In early March of 1970, I finally received my orders for returning home. Not surprisingly, it turned out that a mistake had been made in the preparation of those orders: I was told to report to Saigon for out-processing a day later than I was actually supposed to. When I arrived, I was informed that the plane on which I was scheduled to depart would be leaving in just a couple of hours, that there was no way I could jump through the hoops that I was required to in such short a time, and that I would have to wait for perhaps as much as several days until another plane with an empty seat was available. Desperately wanting to be on "my" airplane, I rushed out of the processing center, found a pedi-cab driver, promised him a large tip if he got me to Tan Son Nhut airbase posthaste. I then tightly gripped all of my possessions while we barreled through the Saigon traffic. We got to the airbase just a few minutes before flight time. I had been told that it would take at least an hour to turn in my military gear and complete the required paperwork in order for me to be on my way. Ignoring proper procedures, I dropped my rifle, flak jacket, helmet, and duffle bag on the tarmac, and raced to the airplane. A sympathetic stewardess allowed me to come aboard—I was instantly infatuated with her! Despite my unorthodox behavior, nobody came to remove me from the plane, and it took off right on time. I heaved a sigh of relief, knowing that this nightmare was about to be over. In contrast to my flight of a year ago (a year that seemed like a lifetime) from the United States to Vietnam, when everybody had been upbeat and enthusiastic, the mood on the flight back to the States was somber and depressing. I think most, if not all, of us were in a state of shock.

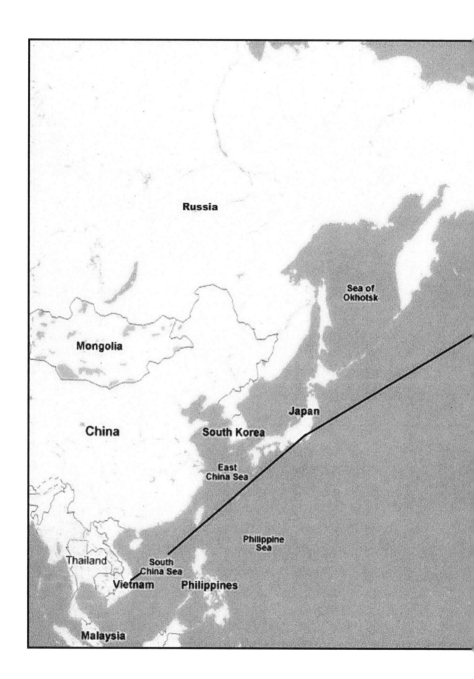

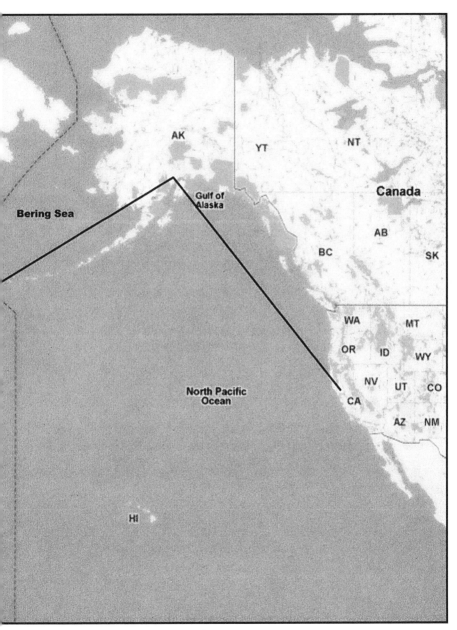

Map of route from Saigon to San Francisco

CHAPTER 5
RETURNING HOME
(MARCH 1970 – JUNE 1973)

The flight back to the States seemed to take forever. With stops in Japan and Alaska, we eventually arrived in San Francisco. The next several days are a total blank for me because I was exhausted, depressed, and completely disoriented. In a daze, I somehow managed to make my way through the out-processing gauntlet, buy some toilet articles and civilian clothes, get on a plane to Boston, and rejoin my wife and daughter.

Everything that had, a year earlier, been comfortable and familiar to me now seemed alien and incomprehensible. I was not able to think clearly, and did not know how to conduct myself in an environment that now seemed so foreign. I actively avoided socializing, and was unwilling to speak to anybody, even my family, about my experiences in Vietnam.

I spent most of my timed holed up in the basement workshop with my two-year-old daughter perched on a high stool next to me, security blanket clutched in her left hand, and her right thumb firmly inserted in her mouth. She didn't say much, but she was intensely present, a great comfort to me, and perhaps the best psychotherapist I could have had at the time. The project that I was working on was the renovation of an old turtleback trunk, and, to this day, that trunk remains my most prized possession. It is symbolic of my having survived a nightmare, and is, in some ways, comparable to my daughter's security blanket.

Somewhere along the line, I received notice from the Commandant of the Fifth Naval District that I had been awarded the Navy Commendation Medal, and he would like to present it to me in a ceremony aboard

his flagship, "Old Ironsides," in Boston Harbor. The idea of putting on a uniform again, or much less of setting foot on a Navy base, made my flesh crawl, so I requested that the medal be mailed to me. I found it odd that I was being awarded such a medal, especially after my being threatened with court martial several times, but I assumed that it made one of my former superior officers look good—a cynical thought, perhaps, but probably accurate. In any event, I gave the medal to my daughter, and it, like all of my other meaningless medals, eventually ended up incorporated into one of her various art projects over the years.

Navy Commendation Medal

Eventually I took a job as treasurer at a private secondary school and moved, with my family, to New Jersey. It was a job for which I was well trained, but didn't much enjoy, because it was primarily one of routine number shuffling, and allowed for very little in the way of creativity or innovation. I didn't ruminate much about Vietnam, but rather coped by compartmentalizing my thoughts and feelings. I found some comfort in my family and in alcohol, but mostly I just felt blank and numb. I preferred that people not know I was a Vietnam Veteran, so I continued to maintain my silence about having served there. Given the sentiments of the time, many people seemed to believe that being a Vietnam Veteran was disgraceful, and treated veterans as if they were pariah. Even those who were well intentioned asked many, many questions that were far too painful for me to answer.

~ ~ ~

In late April of 1970, the United States and South Vietnam invaded Cambodia. Americans were outraged at the expansion of the war into yet another country, and protests erupted on the campuses of America's universities. On May 4th the now infamous Kent State Massacre occurred. Again, the powers-that-be chose to speak euphemistically of the incident as the "Kent State Riots," thereby shifting the blame onto the students. That day, National Guardsmen shot and killed four unarmed students, wounding another nine, at Kent State University in Ohio. Students across the country went on strike—four million students and 450 universities, colleges, and high schools were ultimately involved. Similar violence occurred on other campuses. Through the oppression of my upset, I tried to ignore what was happening, but the horrors of those events added significantly to the festering dismay I was experiencing.

A year later, the students at the school where I was working decided to hold a commemorative rally for those who had been killed in the Kent State Massacre. I decided the time had finally come for me to share my personal experiences, because clearly trying to bury them wasn't working for me, and I volunteered to be a speaker at the rally. While trying to prepare my speech, I continued to draw one blank after another—absolutely nothing would come to me. The day of the rally, I realized that I was going to have to stand up at the podium in front of hundreds of people, open my mouth, and go with whatever came out. I was scheduled to speak for 15 minutes, which I feared would feel like an eternity. As it turned out, I spoke extemporaneously for about 40 minutes. I was so caught up in the moment that I was completely unaware of the world around me and of the passage of time. When I was finished, I had no recollection of what I had said, but I received a standing ovation, so it must have been meaningful. I was dumbfounded.

After my speech, I was approached by representatives of the Vietnam Veterans Against The War (VVAW) and invited to go on speaking tours with them. I was tempted, having been moved by their demonstrations in Washington, D.C. in April 1971, and especially by John Kerry's testimony before the Senate Foreign Relations Committee, but I declined because I knew I wouldn't be able to deal with the crowds, the politics, and the public exposure. In retrospect, I'm very glad that I did decline. While my experiences in Vietnam had shifted my political philosophies from the right to perhaps slightly left of center, the eventual radicalization of the VVAW turned it into an organization that I wanted no part of.

At some point during this time frame, having developed an interest in Fine Art Photography, I decided to participate in an art show of the works of Vietnam Veterans. When I delivered my photographs to a local Veterans of Foreign Wars center, I encountered considerable hostility and vitriol because of a bumper sticker on my car that read, "Question Authority." Feeling isolated, exposed, and vulnerable, I withdrew even further from social contact.

QUESTION AUTHORITY

Bumper Sticker

In June of 1971, the New York Times published "The Pentagon Papers," a history of the United States' political/military involvement in Vietnam from 1945 to 1967. These classified documents were leaked to the press by Daniel Ellsberg, who felt that he could no longer cooperate in concealing from the American people the manipulations and deceits perpetrated on them by their government. The American public was, of course, outraged by the information contained in these revelations. For me, it was just more of the same stuff I already knew. Ellsberg surrendered to authorities and was indicted on charges of stealing and holding secret documents. In May of 1973, charges against him were dismissed when several irregularities in the government's case came to light.

I Love My Country,
But I Fear My Government

Bumper Sticker

While I was no longer on active duty, I was still in the Naval Reserve until my total obligated time in service, which was to end in June of 1971, expired. In June, I wrote to the Bureau of Naval Personnel requesting confirmation of my separation from the service. Naturally, the courtesy of a reply was not extended to me. I wrote again in August, again in September, and again in February of 1972. Still not having received a reply, I wrote to the "Action Line" (a "let us help you" service) of the local newspaper, and they undertook the task of setting things right. They got on it immediately and, within a few weeks, I had my discharge papers. Bravo for Action Line! At least somebody was on my side, for a change.

~ ~ ~

Disturbing emotions continued to haunt me, and I eventually sought psychological counseling. I was diagnosed with Post-Vietnam Stress Syndrome—now known as Post Traumatic Stress Disorder (PTSD). The symptoms of PTSD can be divided into three clusters. The first, the intrusive cluster, includes recurrent uncontrollable recollections of the traumatic event or events, such as frightening dreams or flashbacks. The second, the avoidance cluster, includes attempts to avoid circumstances that might trigger such recollections or flashbacks. To that end, many sufferers withdraw from social contact. The third, the hyper-arousal cluster, involves difficulty sleeping, violent outbursts, and an exaggerated startle response. My symptoms in the first and third clusters were minimal, but my symptoms in the second, avoidance, cluster continued to get progressively worse.

The experience of betrayal of trust and a violation of "what's right" are said to be key elements in stimulating the avoidance/withdrawal symptoms associated with PTSD. My experiences in Vietnam "had taught [me] that the world was a dangerous place ... and an even more disturbing lesson: how dangerous men were."† While in Vietnam, I had reached the point where I "trusted"—that is, believed they would do what they said they would do—the enemy more than I trusted those for whose side I was fighting, and I trusted the South Vietnamese more than I trusted the Americans because at least their corruption, deceit, and manipulation was openly acknowledged. As a result, I developed a high degree of suspicion and distrust toward any kind of authority to which I might be subjugated. Having become aware of the blatant disregard for truth and honor on the part of those in power in our country was an experience I shared with many others, military and civilian alike, and I believe it may have marked a turning point in our national consciousness. I suspect it was as a result of this awareness that we, as a people, lost our faith, our innocence, and our idealism, and became a nation of cynics. (See Appendix B—"Decade Of Disillusionment.")

Certain neurological conditions as well as having experienced a betrayal of trust in one's family of origin are said to make one more susceptible to PTSD and to exacerbate the symptoms. Both were applicable to me, so I was a prime candidate for experiencing the difficulties associated therewith. My inability to trust interfered with all of my relationships, most notably my marriage, and I cut myself off from people more and more. Eventually, my self-isolation reached the

† Conrad, Joseph. *Heart of Darkness.* xii

point where I realized that I couldn't continue to stay married. I could no longer function effectively as a husband or father, and I needed to be alone so as to be able to focus on my own healing. With great sorrow, but believing it was best for all of us, I told my wife that I needed to get a divorce. It wasn't something that I actively *wanted* to do, but it was something I felt that I *had* to do.

After I moved out of our house, I took up residence in a ramshackle old farmhouse located in the middle of nowhere. My furnishings consisted of a mattress on the floor, a folding card table with two folding chairs, a few crates in which to store my clothes, and, of course, my beloved turtleback trunk. I became very much of a recluse, not leaving the house except to occasionally purchase provisions.

One day I developed a bunch of incapacitating symptoms that required my admission to the hospital. The preliminary diagnosis was that of a brain tumor. After several days of extensive testing, the doctors were unable to find anything that confirmed their initial diagnosis, and suggested exploratory surgery. I declined in horror, and opted to return to my hermitage hoping I could just ride the situation out. I was essentially non-functional because I was experiencing significant vertigo, extremely blurred vision, and nausea. I could barely walk, and I wasn't able to read or watch television. Any attempt to stay upright, even in a sitting position, was totally exhausting, and so I spent about 20 hours each day sleeping. I still needed food, of course, but was absolutely alone, with no one to call on for assistance. Struggling to cope, when I needed provisions I would drag myself out of bed first thing in the morning, drive unsteadily at 15 mph to the nearest grocery store, do my shopping (making every effort not to throw up), return to the house, and collapse on my mattress for about 4 hours.

Six months later, after recovery from my physiological symptoms, I decided to see what I could do to effect a recovery from my psychological symptoms as well. To that end, I began an intensive program of psychotherapy, started taking an anti-depressant, and joined an alternative spiritual community. It was slow going, but I was eventually able to reenter the everyday world and to function reasonably effectively. Now, 40 years later, while I still experience many of the avoidance/withdrawal symptoms, I have learned to cope with them—avoiding crowds and noise, getting plenty of alone time and sleep, and maintaining structure, order, routine, and control in my life. Of particular value was giving myself permission to do things in my own idiosyncratic way, and to not be bothered by people thinking of me as an eccentric. I am now able to lead a reasonably contented and productive life.

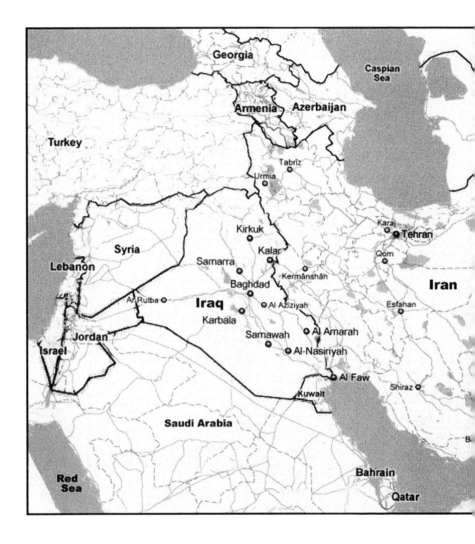

Map of Iraq, Iran, Afghanistan, and Pakistan

CHAPTER 6
AFTERMATH
(JUNE 1973 – JUNE 2011)

The philosopher George Santayana is credited with the saying, "Those who forget history are doomed to repeat it," and also with the saying, "Only the dead have seen the end of war." Those sayings certainly apply to the aftermath of the Vietnam War. As soon as possible, Americans deliberately began the process of forgetting about their nation's longest and most debilitating war, a war that ended in ignominious defeat, a war that showed the United States was not as invincible as we would have liked to believe. Over the succeeding years, other wars, of course, have continued to come along, and with the beginning of the Iraq war in 2003, we embarked on another adventure that couldn't have been more similar to Vietnam if we had intentionally tried to make it so.

That war's beginning was also grounded in deceits perpetrated by the U.S. Government—especially the claims that Iraq possessed weapons of mass destruction, and that Iraq was involved in the attacks on this country of September 11, 2001. Both of those claims have since been definitively proven to be false. As a country, we were again operating under the belief that because we had the *ability* to wage war, we also had the *obligation* to wage war; we were again embracing the dangerous self-delusion that we were on a providential mission to save the rest of the world from itself; we were again attempting to impose our virtues, which we perceived as superior to all other virtues, on others by force. We again invaded another country, not in defense of our own country, but in the name of promoting freedom and democracy; we again began treating the destruction of a civilian population as "collateral damage," and subscribed to the philosophy that, "If it's Iraqi, and if it's dead, then it's an insurgent;" we again heard our government characterize those Americans who did not support the administration's position as being unpatriotic; we again falsely assured our troops that they would be greeted as liberators; we again provided our men with inadequate training and insufficient equipment, kept them in-country beyond their allotted time, and told them to risk their lives for reasons that were repeatedly changed when those reasons were exposed as lies.

During the time that we were deeply involved in that war, public opinion polls showed that more than 50% of Americans were opposed to it, yet neoconservatives within our government pushed for expansion of the war into Afghanistan, and suggested the possibility of air strikes in both Pakistan and Iran. As of this writing (2011), we have a major military involvement in Afghanistan, we are conducting air strikes (theoretically only with unmanned drones, thus giving us "plausible deniability") in Pakistan, and Iran is very much on our potential target list. We seem to be blind to the potential horrific aspects of these policies. Expanding the war in Afghanistan may well make the war in Iraq look like a picnic by comparison; expanding the war into Pakistan could turn Pakistan into the first radical Islamic regime armed with nuclear weapons; strikes on Iran may well result in a wide-spread regional conflict with the potential of drawing Israel into the war.

For the common soldier, in the waging of war today, nothing much seems to have changed from the way things were in Vietnam. Our troops are still inadequately trained and supplied; they still are forced to witness, and sometimes participate in, atrocities; they still experience betrayal at the hands of their superior officers; they still suffer debilitating psychological damage, leading to alcohol and substance abuse, suicides, fraggings, combat refusals, and desertions; they still are poorly supported by the Veterans' Administration on their return home. Perhaps it is unavoidable, but many, if not most, returning veterans will carry with them the scars of war—psychological if not physical—for the rest of their lives. War will never be a cakewalk, and, in the words of General William Tecumseh Sherman from some 130 years ago, "War is Hell!" Nevertheless, I believe that some modicum of constructive change can be effected if the will exists for that to happen.

While nothing much can be done about the fact that "… under pressure and removed from customary restraints, even [the most civilized of men] could give way to destructive impulses rising from the depths of their own natures,"† within the context of the military, there are perhaps a few things that could be done to improve the lot of the regular soldier who has, historically, been used and discarded:

† Conrad, Joseph. *Heart of Darkness.* xii

- Clear-cut goals and objectives for the conduct of each and every war must be established and widely promulgated so the troops know what it is they are fighting for. There is no place for secrecy and deception, except in those circumstances where national security is clearly at stake.

- The length of tours of duty must be clearly stated up front and not extended, except in situations of utmost urgency—in which case, the reason for that urgency must be explained in detail to those affected.

- Training, equipment, supplies, and logistics must be top-notch so the soldiers feel supported, and know they can rely on the powers-that-be to do everything possible to take care of them.

- Every effort must be made to build and maintain unit cohesion so the troops are able to fight alongside and for their buddies, rather than having to go it alone.

- Ethically sound Rules of Engagement must be widely promulgated and all personnel, *at all levels of command*, must be held accountable for following them.

- Procedures must be put into place to guarantee the availability of appropriate judicial avenues to provide legal counsel and guidance for those who refuse to follow orders they believe to be unlawful or unethical.

- The Veterans' Administration must be overhauled so as to provide appropriate guidance, care, and support for those returning veterans who are in need of assistance.

While the above suggestions are obvious, and perhaps somewhat simplistic, they are at least a place to start. War will always be with us; war will always be destructive; war will always wreak havoc on the psyches of military personnel and civilians alike. The experience of all wars can be summed up in the dying words of Kurtz, another major character in Joseph Conrad's *Heart of Darkness*: "The Horror! The Horror!"

Bumper Sticker

APPENDIX A
DEFINING IMAGES

There are a handful of photographic images that, for me, define the context of the war in which I served. In their time, they were ubiquitous in the worldwide news media. While I personally did not take part in any of the events depicted, the images themselves were so powerful that they permanently seared their way into my consciousness. I suspect they had a similar impact on the consciousness of a great many Americans who were born before 1955. I present six of those images here—four of which were awarded the Pulitzer Prize.

Burning Monk In Saigon
Photographer: Malcolm Brown
Date: June 11, 1963
Location: Saigon, South Vietnam
Winner of the Pulitzer Prize
Image accessed via www.famouspictures.org
Image modified for clarity

Tich Quang Duc, a 66 year old Buddhist monk, sat on a cushion in the middle of a circle of other monks and nuns in downtown Saigon. His religious brothers poured gasoline over him as he meditated in the lotus position. With his prayer beads in his right hand, he opened a box of matches, lit one, and was instantly engulfed in flames. He did not move while his body was was being incinerated. He was protesting the religious discrimination against Buddhists in South Vietnam.

Street Execution
Photographer: Eddie Adams
Date: February 1, 1968
Location: Saigon, South Vietnam
Winner of the Pulitzer Prize
Image accessed via www.famouspictures.org
Image modified for clarity

General Nguyen Ngoc Loan used his pistol to execute, with a shot to the head, a Vietcong operative, Nguyen Van Lam, on a street in Saigon. After the shooting, Loan told a group of reporters, "Those guys kill a lot of our people, and I think Buddha will forgive me."

My Lai Massacre

Photographer: Ronald L. Haberle
Date: March 16, 1968
Location: My Lai, South Vietnam
Image accessed via www.commons.wikimedia.org
Image modified for clairty

Operating under Task Force Barker, Charlie Company of the Americal Division entered the village of My Lai expecting to encounter fierce resistance. All they found were old men, women and children. Given that they were in a "free-fire zone" where standing orders were to kill anything that moved, they opened fire and a mass slaughter ensued. The number of people killed was believed to be between 347 (U.S. estimate) and 504 (NVA estimate).

Kent State Massacre
Photographer: John Filo
Date: May 4, 1970
Location: Kent, Ohio, USA
Winner of the Pulitzer Prize
Image accessed via www.en.wikipedia.org
Image modified for clarity

Mary Ann Vecchio, a 14-year-old runaway, kneels in anguish over the body of Kent State student Jeffery Miller, moments after he was shot to death by the Ohio National Guard. The unarmed students had been protesting the U.S. invasion of Cambodia.

Vietnam Napalm Girl
Photographer: Nick Ut
Date: June 8, 1972
Location: Trang Bang, South Vietnam
Winner of the Pulitzer Prize
Image accessed via www.famouspictures.org
Image modified for clarity

This photo of Kim Phuc was taken just after South Vietnamese planes dropped napalm on her village of Trang Bang. She lived only because she tore off her burning clothes. Ut took her to a hospital in Cu Chi, and she survived after 17 surgical procedures.

Vietnam Airlift
Photographer: Huber Van Es
Date: April 29, 1975
Location: Saigon, South Vietnam
Image accessed via www.famouspictures.org
Image modified for clarity

As North Vietnamese Army forces closed in on Saigon, thousands rushed to escape the Communists. The Americans initiated Operation Frequent Wind, which included helicopter evacuations from downtown Saigon. This image, showing the rooftop of the Pittman Apartments where CIA operatives lived, records one of the last flights out. Only twelve or so of those on the rooftop were able to get aboard the helicopter.

APPENDIX B
DECADE OF DISILLUSIONMENT

Back in the 1950s, and perhaps even into the early 1960s, the American populace could appropriately be characterized as "naive, innocent, and trusting." Even though anybody born after 1965 would find reruns of "Leave It To Beaver," "Ozzie And Harriet," and "Father Knows Best" to be ridiculously "out of touch," those shows were pretty effective in depicting the idealism of that era.

All of that changed during the decade from 1964 to 1974 when incident after incident revealed that those in power in our country were operating with a blatant disregard for truth and honor. This quotation from Lord Acton, a British parliamentarian, says it all: "Power tends to corrupt, and absolute power corrupts absolutely. Great men are almost always bad men." Below I present a timeline for that decade, with a few additional years on either side for context, which delineates some of those incidents. By 1975, we were well on our way to becoming a nation of cynics who had a high degree of suspicion and distrust toward power and authority of any kind.

TIMELINE

November, 1960: John F. Kennedy, with running mate Lyndon Johnson, defeats Richard Nixon in the election for the U.S. presidency.

April, 1961: **Bay of Pigs Invasion fails.** CIA-trained Cuban exiles invade Cuba, but don't receive the backing they had anticipated from the U.S., and are defeated.

October, 1962: **Cuban Missile Crisis.** In response to reports of Soviet intermediate range ballistic missiles in Cuba, the United States institutes a naval blockade. Political and military tensions escalate to the point where the world is on the brink of a full-scale nuclear war. The crisis is ultimately averted through behind-the-scenes negotiations in which the Soviet Union agrees to publicly remove its missiles from Cuba in exchange for the United States secretly removing its comparable missiles from Turkey and Italy.

November, 1963: Ngo Dinh Diem, president of South Vietnam is assassinated in a coup d'état staged by Vietnamese Army generals and supported by the United States.

November, 1963: **John F. Kennedy is assassinated** by Lee Harvey Oswald. Suggestions of conspiracy abound. Lyndon Johnson assumes the U. S. presidency.

August, 1964: **Gulf of Tonkin Incident.** Using as a pretext the alleged attack by North Vietnamese torpedo boats on two U.S. Navy destroyers, President Lyndon Johnson arranges for Congress to pass the "Gulf of Tonkin Resolution," which gives him the authority to deploy conventional forces in Southeast Asia without a formal declaration of war.

November, 1964: Lyndon Johnson, with running mate Hubert Humphrey, defeats Barry Goldwater in the election for the U.S. presidency.

February, 1965: The United States begins bombing of North Vietnam.

March, 1965: The first official U. S. combat unit begins fighting in Vietnam.

April, 1965: **Students for a Democratic Society (SDS)** organizes the first large-scale anti-war demonstration, approximately 25,000 strong, in Washington, D.C.

June, 1967:	**Vietnam Veterans Against the War** is established.
January, 1968:	**Tet Offensive.** The North Vietnamese and Viet Cong launch major countrywide attacks against the South Vietnamese, the Americans, and their allies. Although the offensive is a military defeat for the Communists, it is a great political success. It has a profound effect on the U.S. government and shocks the U.S. public, which had been led to believe by its political and military leaders that the Communists were incapable of launching such a massive effort. The majority of Americans turn against the war.
March, 1968:	**My Lai Massacre.** U.S. soldiers of the 1st platoon, "Charlie" Company, of the 1st battalion, 20th Infantry Regiment, 11th Brigade of the Americal Division, under the command of Second Lieutenant William Calley murder somewhere between 347 and 504 unarmed civilians in the Vietnamese village of My Lai.

April, 1968:	**Martin Luther King is assassinated** by James Earl Ray. Suggestions of conspiracy abound.
June, 1968:	**Robert F. Kennedy is assassinated** by Sirhan Sirhan shortly after winning the California and South Dakota primary elections for the Democratic nomination for President of the United States. Suggestions of conspiracy abound.
August, 1968:	**Woodstock Festival.** More than 500,000 people gather at a dairy farm in the Catskill Mountains of New York for an unprecedented three days of peace and music.
November, 1968:	Richard Nixon, with running mate Spiro Agnew, defeats Hubert Humphrey in the election for the U.S. presidency.
July, 1968:	"Vietnamization" of the war begins with the withdrawal of some U.S. military units.
June, 1969:	**Green Beret Affair.** Eight U. S. Special Forces soldiers, including colonel Robert Rheault, commander of all Special Forces troops in Vietnam, are arrested and charged with premeditated murder in the

execution of a suspected Viet Cong double agent. Those charges were quashed by President Nixon in September, 1969.

November, 1969: **Moratorium to End the War in Vietnam.** More than 500,000 demonstrators, the most ever, gather in Washington, D.C. to protest the war.

April, 1970: **Cambodian Invasion.** South Vietnamese and United States military forces invade Cambodia in order to attack the approximately 40,000 North Vietnamese and Vietcong troops who are ensconced in the eastern border regions.

May, 1970: **Kent State Massacre.** While unarmed students at Kent State University in Ohio are demonstrating against the invasion of Cambodia, troops from the Ohio National Guard open fire on them, killing four and wounding another nine. Four million students go on strike and hundreds of educational institutions throughout the country close.

March, 1971:	Lieutenant William Calley is convicted of murder in the My Lai massacre. He is court martialed and originally given a life sentence. Many Americans are outraged at what they perceive to be a scapegoating of Calley by his superior officers. His sentence was commuted by President Nixon, and he served only three and a half years under house arrest.
April 1971:	**Vietnam Veterans Against the War** leads an anti-war demonstration of more than 350,000 people. John Kerry testifies before the Senate Foreign Relations Committee about atrocities committed by Americans in Vietnam.
June, 1971:	**Pentagon Papers published.** Daniel Ellsberg had leaked this Department of Defense history of the United States' political/military involvement in Vietnam to a reporter at the New York Times. The Pentagon Papers "demonstrated, among other things, that the Johnson Administration had systematically lied, not only to the public but also to Congress, about a subject of transcendent national interest and significance."

March, 1972:	**Easter Offensive.** North Vietnamese forces, some 120,000 strong, launch major attacks against several locations in South Vietnam, with the most significant invasion being across the Demilitarized Zone.
June, 1972:	**Watergate scandal.** President Richard Nixon's staff members orchestrate a break-in of the Democratic National Committee headquarters in the Washington, D.C. Watergate office complex, with the intention of discovering the Democrats' political campaign plans. Once the incident comes to light, the Nixon administration attempts to cover up its involvement.
November, 1972:	Richard Nixon, with running mate Spiro Agnew, defeats George McGovern in the election for the U.S. presidency.
March, 1973:	The last remaining American troops are withdrawn from Vietnam.
August, 1973:	As a result of the Case-Church Amendment passed by the U.S. Congress, U.S. military involvement in Vietnam officially ends.

October, 1973:	**Vice President Spiro Agnew resigns** in disgrace, having been accused of corruption and extortion. House Minority Leader, Gerald Ford is appointed Vice President.
August, 1974	**President Richard Nixon resigns** in disgrace, under the threat of impeachment, after the Watergate scandal. Gerald Ford assumes the presidency, pardons Nixon, and appoints Nelson Rockefeller as Vice President.
April, 1975	**Saigon falls.** North Vietnamese forces overrun Saigon, the capital of South Vietnam, thus ending the Vietnam War.

AFTERWORD
BY HARPER SCHANTZ

The above picture of my Dad and me was taken about six months after his return from Vietnam. He was then twenty-seven years old. Today, when I look at his young, seemingly innocent face in that picture, I think of where he had been and all he had been through in the previous couple of years, and I compare his experiences with my own at that age. When I was twenty-seven, I had never been subjected to the atrocities of war; I had never been required to make life-and-death decisions; I had never felt the guilt of knowing that I, however unavoidably, was responsible for the deaths of numerous innocent people; I had never been forced to put my principles on the line at the risk of imprisonment or death; and I had never, in fact, even seen a dead body.

For the purpose of this afterword, however, the biggest psychological difference between my father and myself at the age of twenty-seven, was the nature of the internalized perceptions of the world that each of us held as a result of the differences in our experiences. His perspective was, and continues to be, one of disillusionment, distrust, and cynicism, arising out of the many betrayals he experienced at the hands of those authority figures who he had counted on to support him, back him up, and minimize his risks while he was serving his country.

I, on the other hand, would describe myself at that age as having been unrelentingly (and, yes, often unrealistically) optimistic and idealistic, despite, or possibly because of, the fact that my own experience of life, on a very personal level, had been less than ideal. This unrealistic attitude was probably a reflexive survival mechanism I developed to counter grief, loss, and disillusionment. I think, on the other hand, that my tenacious belief in the basic goodness of humanity and the potential for positive change is innate. While being well aware of the suffering that goes on in the world, I am still convinced that it is possible to turn things around—that each and every one of us has the power to make a positive change.

My idealism was fostered, at least in part, by the teenage babysitters I had as a young child in the early 1970's. Their attitudes and lifestyles had a profound effect on me. They were the hippies that I knew, and I idolized them—their long hair, their music, their peace symbols and lava lamps, their way of doing their own thing and not letting society's dictates inhibit them, but, most of all, their passion for a cause—peace and freedom—and their commitment to making their dream a reality. I remember them talking about rallies and demonstrations, and wishing I could go, but of course I was far too young. That didn't stop me, however, from vicariously taking it all in. I now realize that having had this early exposure to a group of young people who believed they had the power to make a difference, firmly implanted such possibilities in my mind, and, without a doubt, shifted the course of my life.

The 1970's were a golden decade for my generation—a time of unprecedented freedom and independence for middle-class American children. We were the first of the latch key kids, as more and more women joined the work force. Groups of us roamed about freely on bicycles and skateboards after school, knowing that our whereabouts wouldn't be questioned unless we failed to show up for dinner. In that case, the neighborhood phone tree would be activated, and we would all be rounded up in a matter of minutes, because, back then, neighbors kept an eye out for one another. Consequently, we couldn't get away with much mischief, and so we were generally well behaved and respectful of others and their property.

Rather than engendering a feeling of resentment, this awareness of being "watched over," and yet left to our own devices, fostered a sense of safety and security, while at the same time allowing us to develop self-sufficiency, resourcefulness, and responsibility. The older kids looked out for the younger ones, we got to do our own thing, and, if we needed help, there were any number of doors we knew we could knock on and some adult would provide us with assistance. It was a time when community was a substantive reality, rather than just an evanescent concept.

Ours has been called the "Brady Bunch" generation, a reference to the popular 1970's TV sitcom about a couple, both of whom have embarked upon their second marriage, each with three children in tow. While still presenting a rather idealized version of family life in that era, the show was considerably more realistic than the sitcoms of the 1950's and 1960's—dealing as it did with a non-traditional family, and presenting interpersonal and sociological issues that required attention. It was definitely a reflection of our times, with divorce rates rising, and non-traditional families becoming more and more common. Given that it addressed problematic issues, rather than portraying life as always being a bowl of cherries, it evidenced a cultural willingness to more honestly address reality.

Nevertheless, it was a time before anyone thought about razor blades in Halloween treats, before random abductions of young people appeared regularly on the evening news, before bombs and guns started showing up in the schools. Many of us who grew up during that era in suburban or rural areas never even locked our doors. It was, in many ways, an idyllic time to be a child, and one that most kids today would have difficulty imagining, given the graphic violence, blatant sexuality, and online predators to which they are now regularly exposed. It was a time before "the innocence of childhood" ceased to have any meaning.

The 1980's proved to be a rude awakening for me. As I became increasingly aware of the disturbing changes in the world around me, I realized that those who I'd previously admired and looked up to had become, for the most part, materialistic yuppies, too caught up in climbing the corporate ladder and advancing their own status to concern themselves with the state of the world at large. They no longer served as effective role models for me, and I felt as if I had no guidance or support as I tried to find my place in society.

By adolescence, I was experiencing major depression, and had become completely cut off from my peers. I began treatment in psychotherapy and a course of antidepressants, but nothing seemed to help. That period of time was devastatingly painful for me. My psychotherapist suggested that my parents' divorce when I was six years old—fallout from my Dad's experience in Vietnam—might have been the underlying cause of my depression. At the time, I had difficulty believing that the emotions I was experiencing nearly a decade later could be related, but I now understand the connection, and depression is an issue that I still struggle with.

In the fall of my tenth-grade year, my Dad took me to the Maine seacoast for a weekend of much needed R&R. I will always remember the night that, in a little lobster shack (which, at that time of year, we had almost completely to ourselves), he shared with me the full story of his time in Vietnam. Over the years, I had heard bits and pieces in the form of anecdotes, always presented with a humorous spin, but that night he spoke to me as an adult, and told me his real truth about his experience of the war. He told me that the many ways in which those experiences had affected him had severely undermined his ability to function in society, especially in the roles of husband and father. He expressed his deep regret that my mother, my brother, and I had been so adversely affected, and he acknowledged that we were casualties of the war, just as much as any wounded veterans—only, in our cases, no Purple Hearts had been awarded.

Having, from the perspective of a very young child, "lost" my father to Vietnam; having experienced the confusion and pain of recognizing that the Daddy who came home was a very different Daddy than the one I had known before he had gone away; having osmosed, in the sponge-like way that young children do, the emotions that took so much of his energy to repress, and feeling that it was somehow my job to make everything better; having been through the undoing that his personal trauma caused our family; and then, again, having lost him when my parents ultimately divorced, grief became, for me, a familiar companion.

It took a lot of encouragement from me to get my Dad to write this book. He was concerned that doing so would reopen any number of old emotional wounds that he would prefer not to deal with. I suggested to him that exploring those issues from the perspective of forty years' hindsight might be less painful than he anticipated, and could actually be quite therapeutic for him. Moreover, I explained to him that it might be very useful to me, by helping me to achieve closure on that particular chapter of my life. I also told him that the book would one day be a valuable legacy for his grandson, my nephew, Brendan—one that would help him to understand who his grandfather was and what he was all about. Finally, I expressed the opinion that the insights he had to offer could prove to be helpful to all veterans—not just those who had served in Vietnam, but also those who had served in Iraq, Afghanistan, and elsewhere.

It remains to be seen as to what this book will have to offer for Brendan, or what value it might hold for other veterans. For my Dad, it was rough going for a while. He found that writing it was stressful and depressing, and it may even have exacerbated the cardiac issues he had been dealing with. In the final analysis, however, he seems to have moved through all of that, and writing the book appears to have had some real healing value for him. For myself … well, it seems to be "a work in progress." In helping him to edit this book, and in writing this afterword, I came to realize that it wasn't just my parents' divorce that was the underlying cause of my depression. I seem to have empathically taken on the emotional content of my Dad's experiences as my own, and that is definitely an unresolved issue for me. Presumably, that is something I need to focus on in my own psychotherapy so as to achieve the final closure I had hoped for.

Santa Fe, NM
February, 2012

GLOSSARY

Army unit sizes:

Unit Type	Strength	Commanded By
Division	10,000 – 15,000	2-Star General
Regiment	3,000 – 5,000	Colonel
Battalion	300 – 1,300	Lt. Colonel
Company	80 – 225	Captain
Platoon	26 – 55	2nd Lieutenant

Military officer ranks:

Pay Grade	Army Rank	Navy Rank
O-7 to O-10	General	Admiral
O-6	Colonel	Captain
O-5	Lt. Colonel	Commander
O-4	Major	Lt. Commander
O-3	Captain	Lieutenant
O-2	1st Lieutenant	Lieutenant JG
O-1	2nd Lieutenant	Ensign

Ambush: A military tactic in which the aggressors (the ambushing force) take advantage of concealment and the element of surprise to attack an unsuspecting enemy from hidden positions.

Black Intelligence: The covert gathering of military and political information, the nature of which, or the methodologies employed, having political implications that would be so disruptive to the relations between two countries that the operatives would be disavowed by their host country if caught. See also, "intelligence."

Body Count: The total number of people (usually specifically referring to the enemy) killed in a particular event. In combat, body count is often based on the number of confirmed kills, but occasionally on only an estimate.

Coccidiomycosis: Also known as "San Joaquin Valley Fever," coccidiomycosis is a fungal disease that causes an influenza-like illness. It has been considered by the U.S. military for use as a biological warfare weapon.

Collateral Damage: Damage that is unintended or incidental to the intended outcome. The phrase is often used as a euphemism for civilian casualties in a military action.

Catch-22: A logical paradox arising from a situation in which an individual needs something that can only be acquired with an action that will lead him to that very situation he is already in; therefore, the acquisition of this thing becomes logically impossible. Catch-22s are often spoken of with regard to rules, regulations, procedures, or situations in which one has knowledge of being or becoming a victim, but has no control over it occurring.

Fragging: The act of attacking, with intent to kill, a superior in one's chain of command. Killing is most often effected by means of a fragmentation grenade, hence the term.

Friendlies: Those who are other than enemy combatants, specifically allied troops and presumed innocent civilians.

Free-Fire Zone: A specific designated area into which any weapon system may be fired without the need to coordinate with other allied military units. In Vietnam, it was assumed that all "friendlies" had been cleared from the area, and that anyone remaining could be considered an enemy combatant. "Standing orders" were that anything moving in a free-fire zone was to be killed. See also, "friendlies," and "standing orders."

Firing Clearance: Authorization given to permit the firing of weapons within a specified area. By giving clearance, the authorizing unit certified that they had no friendlies in that area.

Geneva Conventions: A collection of treaties and protocols that established the standards of international law for humanitarian treatment of victims of war. The articles of the Fourth Geneva Convention extensively defined the basic rights of prisoners, both civilian and military, during war, established protections for the wounded, and established protections for the civilians in and around a war zone.

Ho Chi Minh Trail: A logistical system that ran from North Vietnam to South Vietnam through Laos and Cambodia in support of Vietcong and North Vietnamese Army operations in South Vietnam.

The trail was not a single route, but rather a complex maze of truck routes, paths for foot and bicycle traffic, and river transportation systems.

Intelligence (Military): The gathering, analysis, and dissemination of military and political information for the purpose of providing military commanders with guidance and direction in support of their operational decisions. See also, "black intelligence."

Interdiction: The act of delaying, disrupting, or destroying enemy forces or supplies en route to a battle area.

Medevac: An abbreviation for "Medical Evacuation," medevac is the timely and efficient movement and en route care provided by medical personnel to the wounded being evacuated from the battlefield, usually to a military hospital.

M-16 Rifle: The standard service rifle of the U.S. military during the Vietnam War, the M-16 fires the 5.56x45 mm NATO cartridge on either semi-automatic or full-automatic.

M-79 Grenade Launcher: A single-shot, shoulder-fired, break action, grenade launcher that fires a 40x46 mm grenade.

Nuremberg Principles: A set of international guidelines for determining what constitutes a war crime. Of particular relevance is Principle IV, which states that, "The fact that a person acted pursuant to orders of his Government or superior does not relieve him from [personal] responsibility under international law, provided a moral choice was in fact possible to him."

PBR: See "River Patrol Boat."

PCF: See "Swift Boat."

Pedi-cab: A human-powered type of tricycle (rickshaw) designed to carry passengers for hire with the passengers seated in front and the driver seated behind.

River Patrol Boat (PBR): The river patrol boat was used in the Mekong Delta to stop and search river traffic in an attempt to disrupt enemy weapons shipments. With a fiberglass hull and powered by a water-jet engine, it had a length of 32', a beam of 11', and a draft of 2', and was designed to operate in confined spaces.

Sampan: A relatively flat-bottomed wooden boat, often used for fishing, generally 11.5' to 14.8' in length, propelled by poles, oars, or outboard motors. Some sampans included a small shelter on board and were used as a permanent habitation on inland waters.

Search And Destroy: A military strategy involving the insertion of ground troops, generally by helicopter, into hostile territory with the objective of searching out the enemy, destroying them, and withdrawing immediately thereafter.

Standing Order: An order of indefinite duration, binding upon all personnel affected, the purpose of which is to enforce a policy or procedure unique to a military unit's specific circumstances. It differs from a direct order in that the actor is not explicitly named, nor is that (or whom) which is to be acted upon. Standing orders are general and vague, since the exact circumstances for execution occur in the future under unknown circumstances.

Swift Boat (PCF): These Fast Patrol Craft were all-aluminum shallow-draft vessels initially used for close inshore interdiction work along the coast of Vietnam. They later worked the interior waterways interdicting Vietcong movement of arms and munitions, and inserting SEAL teams for counterinsurgency operations. They were somewhat over-sized for operations in the canals, having a length of 50', a beam of 13', and a draft of 4'.

Unlawful Order: An order that is patently illegal, for example one that directs the commission of a crime. While military personnel are required to disobey an unlawful order, an order requiring the performance of a military duty or act is inferred to be lawful, and it is disobeyed at the peril of the subordinate. Some orders may be considered legal at the national level but illegal at the international level, so an individual who is given such an order is presented with a classic Catch-22. See also, "Catch-22."

Yellow Journalism: Journalism that treats news in an unprofessional or unethical fashion, including distortion, exaggeration, and sensationalism.

Vietnam Veterans Against The War (VVAW): A non-profit national veterans' organization, founded in 1967 to campaign for peace, justice, and the rights of all United States military veterans. John Kerry, later a candidate for U.S. president, was probably its best-known member. Despite its relatively small membership, the VVAW was, for a few years, widely considered to be among the most influential anti-war organizations of that era. The VVAW eventually became radicalized and lost much of its public support.

Volunteer: To offer oneself voluntarily for some service or undertaking. In the military, this concept is often distorted, and a "request for volunteers" is considered to be tantamount to a direct order.

Yippies: Founded in 1967, the Yippies were a radically youth-oriented and countercultural revolutionary offshoot of the free speech and anti-war movements. They adopted the name "Youth International Party" to give themselves more credibility in the media. They have been described as a highly theatrical, anti-authoritarian, and anarchistic youth movement of "symbolic politics."

SELECTED BIBLIOGRAPHY

Belknap, M.R. 2002. *The Vietnam War on Trial.* Lawrence, KS. University Press of Kansas

Bilton, M. and K. Sim. 1992. *Four Hours in My Lai.* New York. Penguin.

Coleman, P. 2006. *Flashback.* Boston. Beacon.

Conrad, J. 1980. *Heart of Darkness.* Norwalk, CT. Easton.

Cortright, D. 1975. *Soldiers In Revolt.* Chicago. Haymarket.

Ellsberg, D. 2003. *Secrets.* New York. Penguin.

Golding, W. 1954. *Lord of the Flies.* New York. Penguin.

Hunt, A. E. 1999. *The Turning.* New York. New York University Press.

Jamail, D. 2009. *The Will To Resist.* Chicago. Haymarket.

Karnow, S. 1983. *Vietnam: A History.* New York. Penguin.

Mangold, T. and J. Penycate. 1985. *The Tunnels of Cu Chi.* New York. Random House.

Oberdorfer, D. 2001. *Tet!: The Turning Point in the Vietnam War.* Baltimore. Johns Hopkins University Press.

Robbins, J. S. 2010. *This Time We Win.* New York. Encounter.

Sheehan, N. 1988. *A Bright Shining Lie.* New York. Modern.

INDEX

ABOUT THE AUTHOR

Then   *Now*

David Ritchey is currently retired from his former vocations of hypnotherapist and fine arts photographer. He now spends most of his time writing about a variety of subjects that have, over the course of his lifetime, fascinated him.

His previous books include: *The H.I.S.S. of the A.S.P.: Understanding the Anomalously Sensitive Person* (about the neuropsychology of paranormal experiences), *The Magic of Digital Fine Art Photography* (a collection of his photographs), *26 Card Tricks* (about magic performed with playing cards), *Something About SCRABBLE™* (a minimalist approach to excelling at the game), and *Why We Are Fascinated By Dogs* (an inquiry into canine consciousness, intelligence, temperament, and extraordinary abilities). He is now working on a rewrite of *The H.I.S.S. of the A.S.P.*, tailored specifically for the layperson.

He lives with his golden retriever, Katherine, in Bucks County, Pennsylvania. He has two grown children, Harper and Mac, and a grandson, Brendan.